COLORED PENCIL
FAST TECHNIQUES

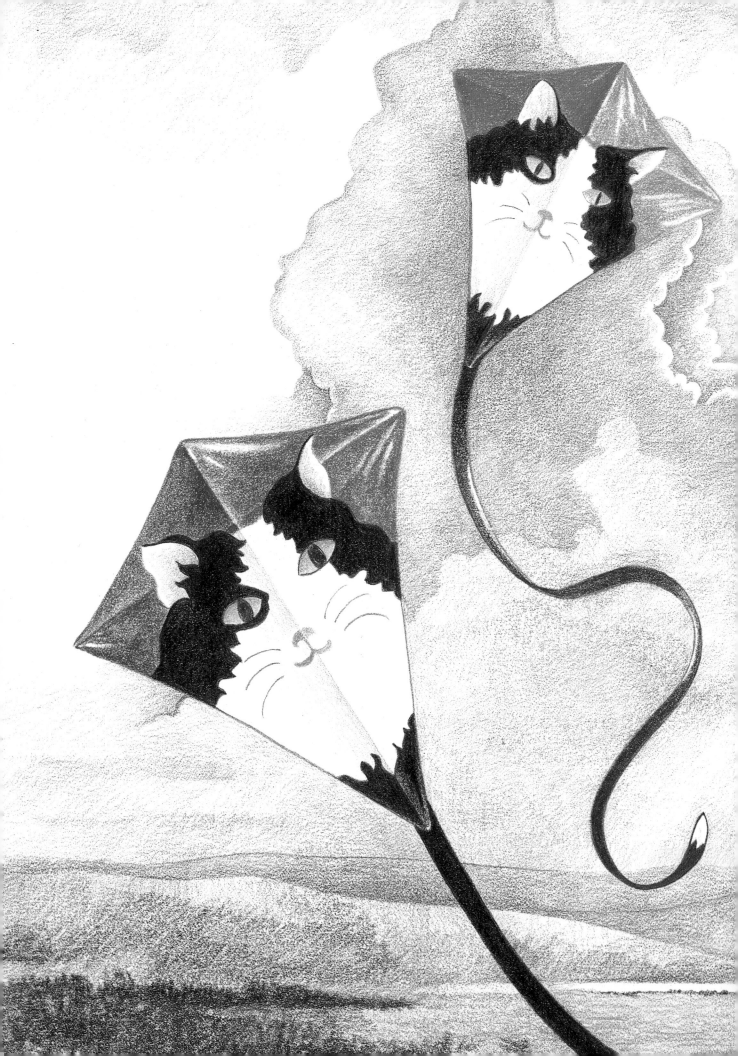

COLORED PENCIL
FAST TECHNIQUES

Bet Borgeson

Photography by Edwin Borgeson

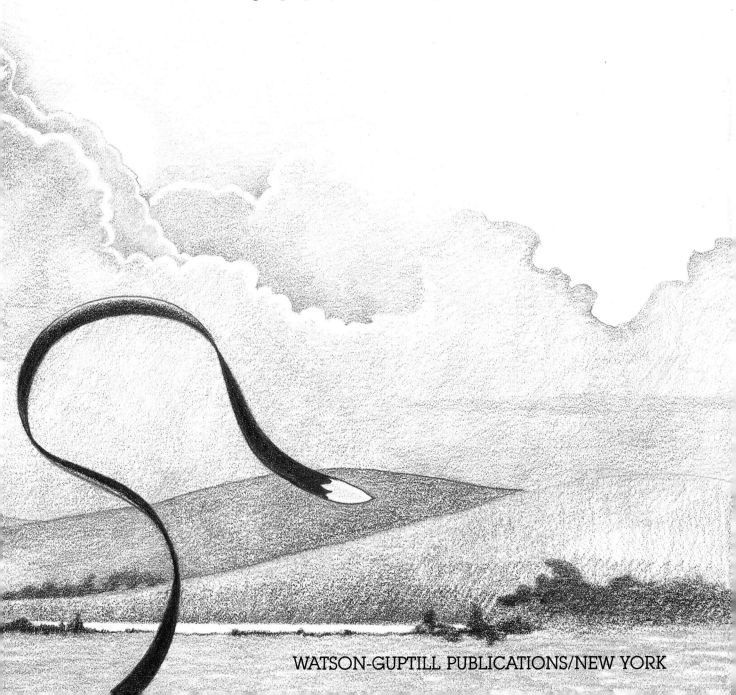

WATSON-GUPTILL PUBLICATIONS/NEW YORK

Other books by Bet Borgeson:
The Colored Pencil
Color Drawing Workshop

First published 1988 in the United States and Canada by Watson-Guptill
Publications, a division of Billboard Publications, Inc., 1515 Broadway,
New York, N.Y. 10036.

Library of Congress Cataloging-in-Publication Data

Borgeson, Bet.
    Colored pencil fast techniques.

    Includes index.
    1. Colored pencil drawing—Technique. I. Title.
NC892.B68 1988   741.2′4   87-34631
ISBN 0-8230-0760-X

Distributed in the United Kingdom by Phaidon Press Ltd., Littlegate
House, Ebbe's St., Oxford

Manufactured in Japan

First printing, 1988

4 5 6 7 8 9 10/93 92

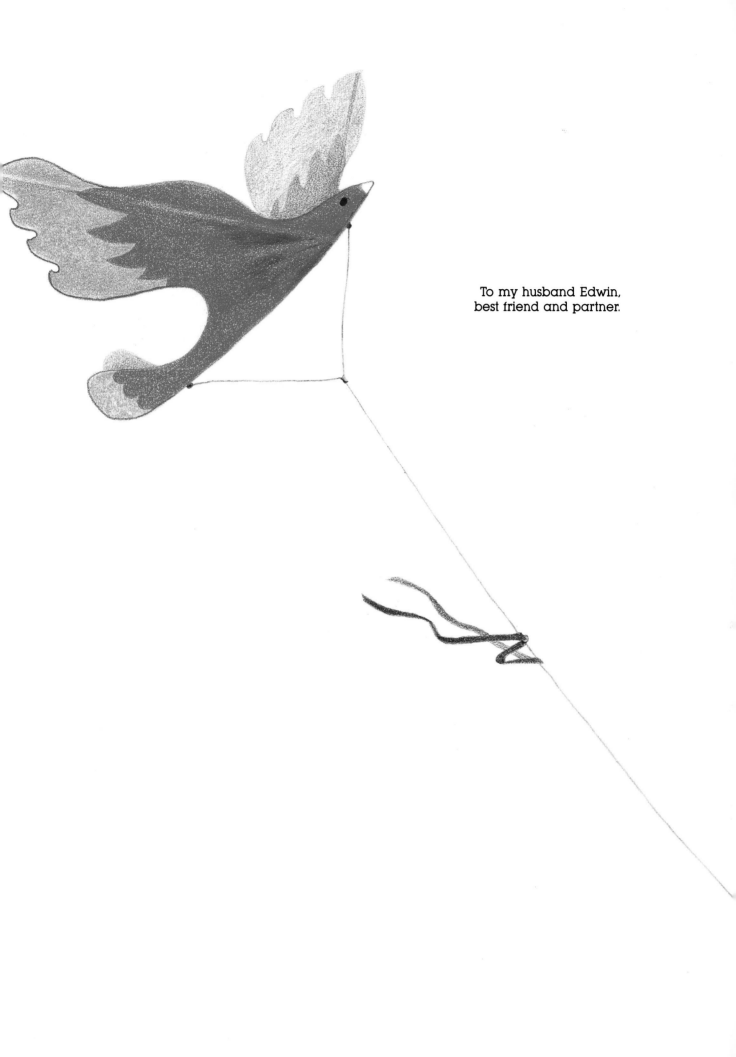

To my husband Edwin,
best friend and partner.

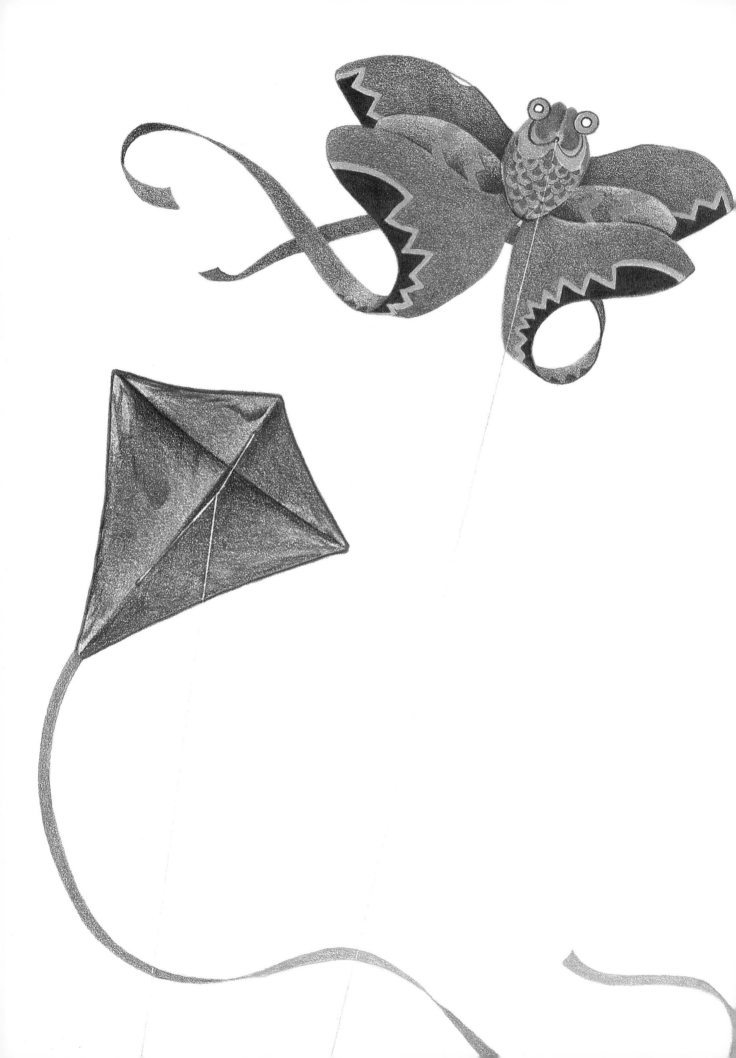

CONTENTS

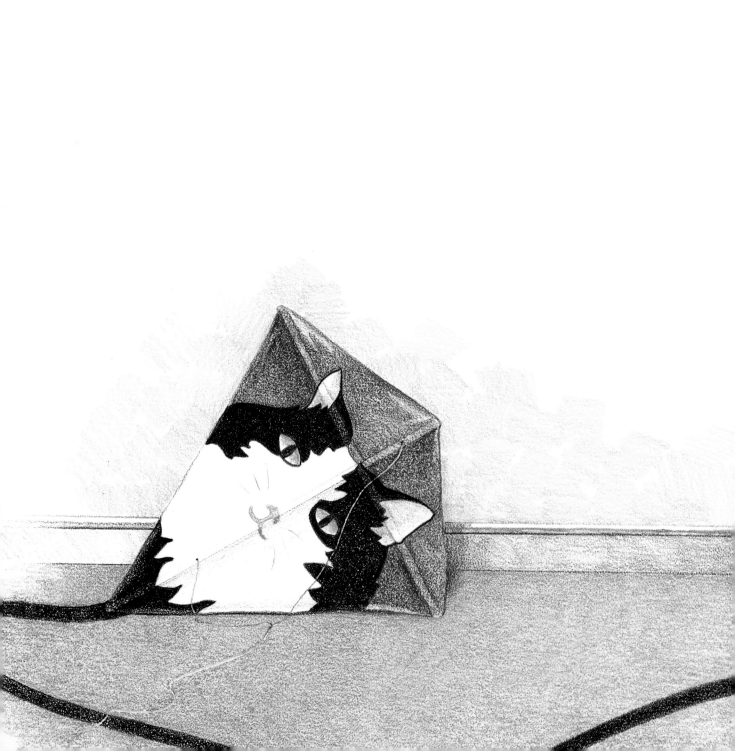

PREFACE

This collection of techniques for working faster with colored pencils is offered as a varied menu of opportunities—ideas from which to pick and choose, depending on one's own temperament, style, and drawing needs. All are anchored firmly in the assumption that quality must never be compromised for speed. Along with increased spontaneity and dramatic savings in time, these techniques will also be found to offer the option of working much larger.

In the appendixes are a series of newly developed color charts, presented here for the first time. They are designed to help in seeing the color properties of individual colored pencils and to enable a faster selection of pencils for specific drawing and color mixing needs. The basic pencils used here and throughout the text are Prismacolor colored pencils.

My thanks are due to many people for direct as well as indirect help and encouragement with this project. One of them is artist and professor Richard Muller, of Portland State University, who provided invaluable insights and suggestions regarding the color charts in the appendixes.

I am grateful too for three kinds of help from three businessmen, none of whom know one another, whose lives touch art in three very separate ways. I want to thank Arnold Ashkenazy, a spellbinder who makes art itself seem the greatest possible adventure. I want to thank Kenneth Peck, an inventor and entrepreneur whose strong words of advice helped move this effort from idea to reality. And I want to thank Arnold J. Hyatt, who introduced me unforgettably to a view of confrontation as a positive rather than a hostile force—as ultimately the truest economy of action.

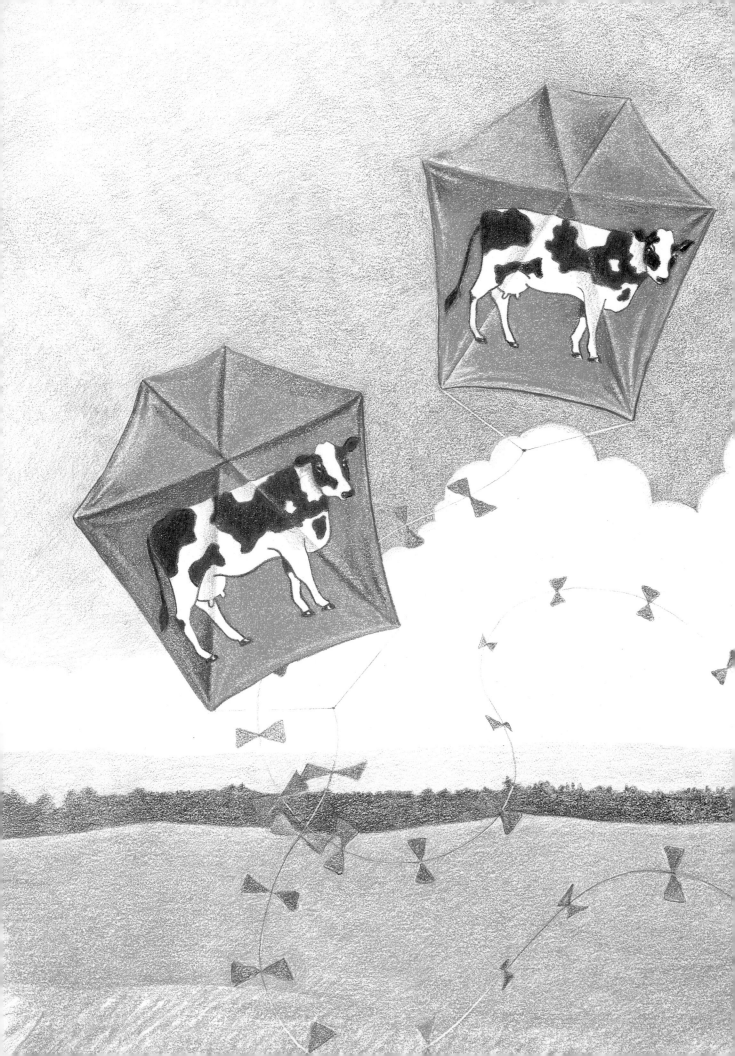

FASTER COLOR APPLICATION

Color drawing consists of two major technical tasks: the drawing and the simultaneous color application. Part One explains and demonstrates pivotal concepts for reducing the excessive time often used to apply color, allowing a better balance between the two tasks. After reviewing what we usually want to accomplish with basic layering techniques, we will consider chapter by chapter the various ways of achieving very similar results at far less cost in time and with more vitality.

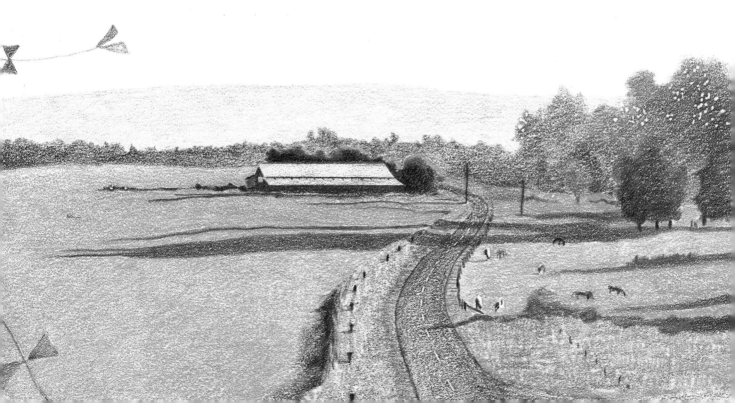

1

A BASIC LAYERING STRATEGY

The concept of layering is basic to colored pencil drawing. This stacking up of one semitransparent colored line or tone over another is how modern colored pencils achieve the subtle, hue-laden complexities for which they are best known.

But those of us who draw with colored pencils soon learn something else about layering: We find it takes time, and frequently too much time. Many of us get caught up in the fascination of superimposing colors on paper, of seeing them almost magically shift and change—and the hours slide by as we layer too much and too extensively.

The truth is, we ourselves often make our colored pencil work more time-intensive than it need be. We can save a great deal of drawing time—as much as 50 percent of our layering time in particular—if we want to. It may require a changed attitude and a new strategy. But it won't lessen the quality of our color mixtures, which will be just as expressively developed, nor the overall quality of our work, which more likely will improve.

As a beginning toward saving time at colored pencil drawing, consider the four major reasons for layering with colored pencils:

1. To reduce the uncomplicated brilliance of single pencil colors. (Painters also do this to reduce the harshness of single pigments.)

2. To mix and arrive at new colors precisely suited to a personal need.

3. To modulate color, and to otherwise add dimension, complexity, and richness within each color passage.

4. To create or change texture by a manipulation of surface.

Our basic strategy for speeding up our colored pencil drawing will hinge directly on a firm understanding of why we layer, of what we are truly trying to achieve, and of how we can depart from conventional layering toward this end.

ORNAMENTS #2
Colored pencil on medium-grained paper,
17″ × 12″ (43.2 cm × 30.5 cm). Private
collection.

The elements in this small drawing were drawn with from one to three layers of color, yet it is difficult to distinguish exactly which layers are single colors and which are not. My idea was to use complex layering only where really needed, with other, less time-intensive methods of color mixing elsewhere. This approach can save a great deal of the time we so often lose in over-layering.

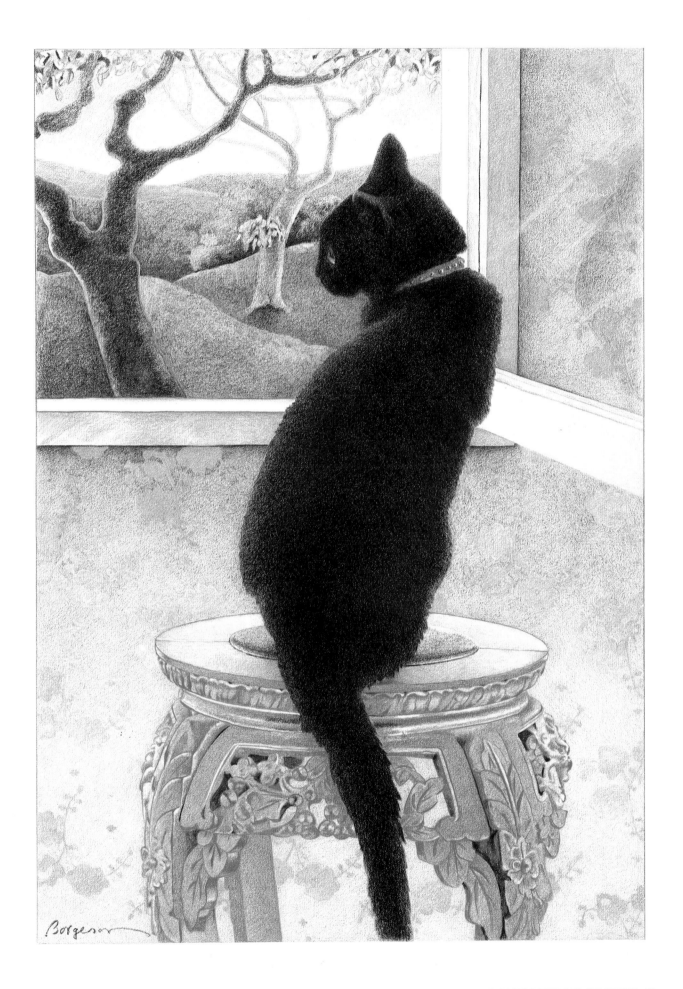

2

FAST-WORKING PAPERS

A drawing paper can itself contain a built-in speed factor. The choice of one brand of paper over another can actually produce a dramatic difference in the speed of colored pencil work.

Differences in paper speed relate to the way a pencil's color is delivered to a paper's surface. When pencil strokes are applied fairly rapidly to a medium-grained paper, with medium pencil pressure, the pigment is first deposited on the highest ridges or hills of the paper's surface. Covering the paper more thoroughly—filling in the white flecks that are the valleys—requires either using heavy pencil pressure, with its attendant wax buildup, or working the pencil slowly into the valleys with a very sharp point.

Fast-working papers speed up this process because they have a somewhat softer and slightly less rigid-toothed surface than other papers. These characteristics make it possible to accomplish very rapid color saturation, even with a dull pencil point and only moderately heavy pencil pressure.

You can find your own fast-working paper by seeking out one that is soft, but not so soft that it cannot hold the edge of a sharp, crisp line. Be sure that you test both sides. Your "right" side may be someone else's wrong side. Above all, don't try to judge fast papers by merely looking at or touching them. The real test lies in drawing on them with your own pencils.

These three simplified schematic views show how colored pencil pigment is transferred to paper.

With ordinary medium-grained papers and moderate pencil pressure, pigment is deposited on the relatively rigid hills of the paper's tooth. This results in a white-flecked appearance that is not always desirable.

To reduce the fleck and gain more color saturation—still with moderate pencil pressure—pigment must be deposited in the paper's valleys with a sharp pencil point.

With a softer, fast-working paper, tonal applications of pigment with moderate pencil pressure compress hills and valleys together. This means that a well-saturated passage of color can be applied rapidly, with no particular need for a sharp point.

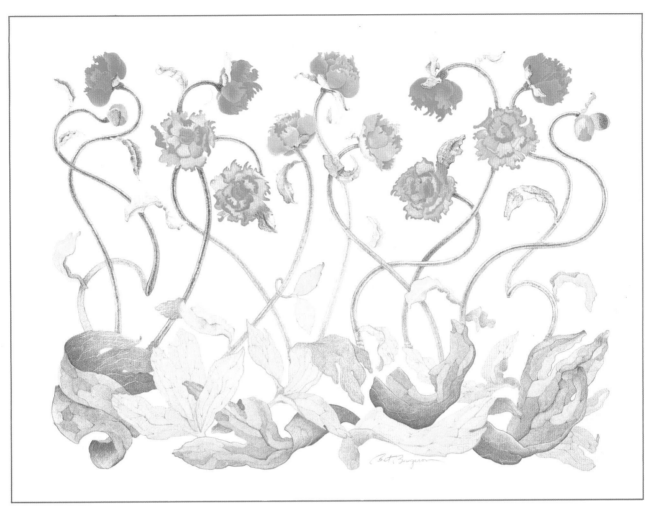

WHITE FLORAL
Colored pencil on Rising museum board,
32″ × 40″ (81.3 cm × 101.6 cm). Private
collection.

*Rising museum board provides a
fast-working surface for medium to
heavy pencil pressure.*

Polyester Film—Another Fast Surface

*Cronaflex—a translu-
cent, neutral pH, poly-
ester tracing film,
frosted on both
sides—may be the
fastest surface of all
for colored pencil
work. Pencil pigments
can be applied either
linearly or tonally to
its frosted surfaces;
they immediately ap-
pear dense and satu-
rated. Visible
granularity is prac-
tically nonexistent,
and the finished look
with colored pencils is
much like that of a
painting.*

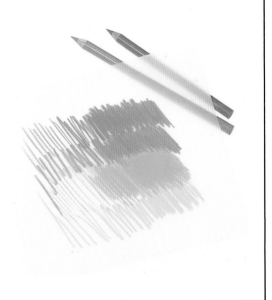

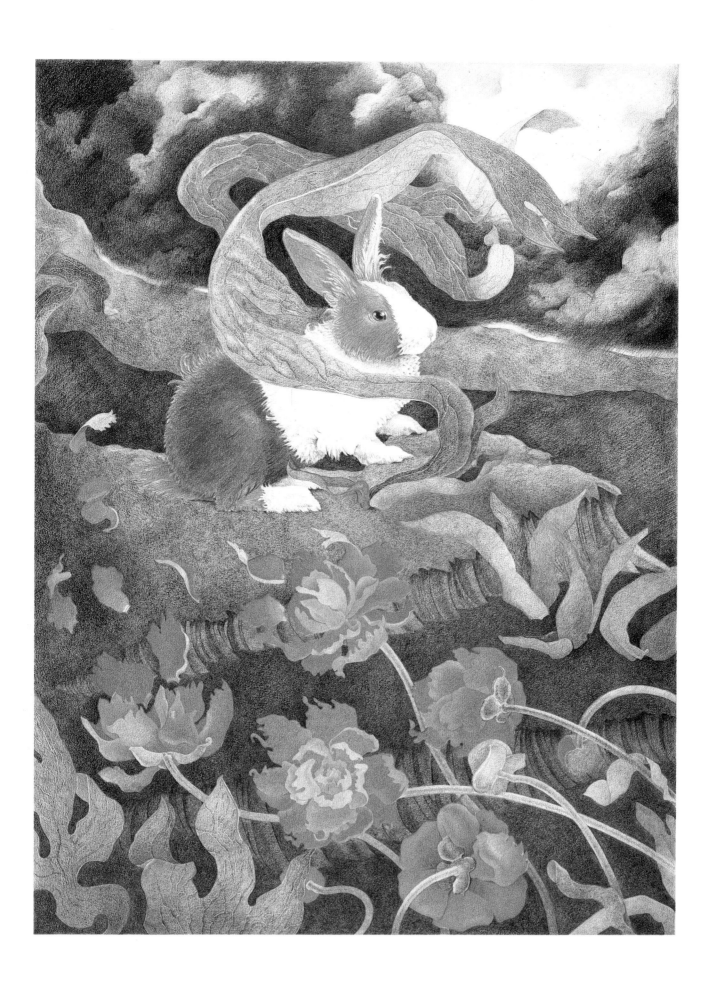

3

A TWO-LAYER APPROACH

A sure way to save time at colored pencil layering is to simply use fewer layers. Imagine, for example, that you are about to begin a drawing and know at the start that you will be limited to no more than two layers of color.

With this kind of limitation, it becomes important to start thinking immediately of how to best use your two layers. Our basic reasons for layering, remember, are to subdue brilliant colors, to mix new colors, to modulate colors, and to develop surface textures. You can do a great deal in all four of these areas with only two layers.

You may also want to remember some color theory that applies to pairs. Mixing two bright colors will reduce the brilliance of both. With analogous colors, the reduction will be very subtle; with near-complementary colors, it will be pronounced. By combining two low-intensity colors, you can attain a look of complexity similar to that achieved by mixing several colors. To appraise individual colors, use the color charts in the Appendix. With them, you can quickly pinpoint hue, value, and intensity (also called saturation or chroma) characteristics.

Try a two-layer approach wherever you can. It doesn't mean giving up third and fourth layers forever. What it does mean is using your extra layers only for key color passages or particular emphasis, rather than as a quiet thief of your time.

HERO
Colored pencil on two-ply Strathmore bristol board, 24″ × 19″ (61.0 cm × 48.3 cm).
Collection of Mr. and Mrs. Robert P. Cummins, Chicago, Illinois.

In this drawing, no more than two layers of color were used except for the rabbit's fur and one of the distant hills. Three layers were used for these areas.

Layering two bright analogous colors (top) results in a subtle reduction in brilliance. Bright near-complementary colors (center) become almost neutral. When two low-intensity colors are layered (bottom), the result always appears to contain more than two colors.

Step-By-Step
A RECONSTRUCTED DRAWING

This reconstruction of a drawing illustrates a two-layer approach. *Cat and Tulips* (below) was originally drawn with as many as five layers of color in some places. However, I believe I could have achieved almost the same effect with much less color. My plan will be to look carefully at the original color layers and from these plan a very similar two-layer version. Also, I would like to brighten the flowers this time and generally increase the contrast between the various elements.

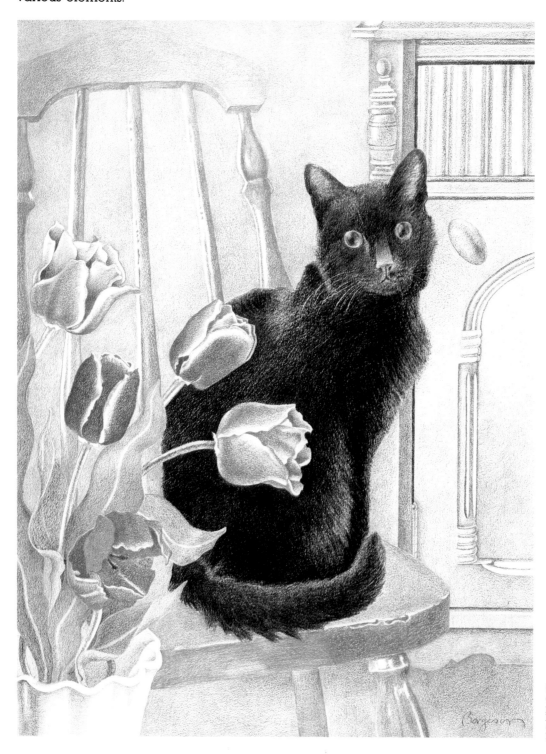

CAT AND TULIPS
Colored pencil on two-ply Strathmore bristol board, 18″ × 13½″ (45.7 cm × 34.3 cm). Private collection.

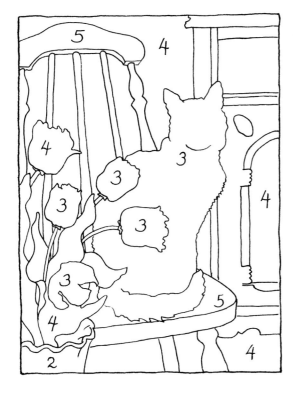

This sketch maps the approximate number of pencil layers originally used. The extensive color mixing resulted in an overall color scheme of low intensity. This is not of itself an undesirable scheme, and it is an important factor in the drawing's mood. But a low-intensity scheme need not rely solely on the number of layers used. It can, in fact, be more quickly achieved with simple color mixtures that are themselves of low intensity.

Here are some of the drawing's original color mixtures and the new mixtures planned to replace them:

Background:
Original: 931 Purple, 933 Blue Violet, 956 Light Violet, and 949 Silver.
New: 931 Purple and 949 Silver. This will retain the silver-purple quality, and the silver alone will cool the purple.

Chair:
Original: 932 Violet, 937 Tuscan Red, 942 Yellow Ochre, 943 Burnt Ochre, and 949 Silver.
New: 943 Burnt Ochre and 956 Light Violet. The burnt ochre seems closest to the original hue. The light violet will reduce the rawness of the burnt ochre and relate the chair's color to the background.

Cabinet:
Original: 902 Ultramarine, 903 True Blue, 929 Pink, and 932 Violet.
New: 903 True Blue and 931 Purple. The true blue will work best here, and a single purple can replace the pink and violet.

Cat:
Original: 901 Indigo Blue, 931 Purple, and 937 Tuscan Red.
New: 901 Indigo Blue and 937 Tuscan Red. The purple will be dropped to reduce the purple cast of the original color scheme.

Flowers:
Original: 923 Scarlet Lake, 924 Crimson Red, 930 Magenta, 931 Purple, 937 Tuscan Red, and 949 Silver, used in combinations of three or four layers.
New: 923 Scarlet Lake, 924 Crimson Red, 930 Magenta, and 931 Purple, used in combinations of two layers. Dropping the Tuscan red and silver and using no more than two layers will help increase the brightness of this area, as planned.

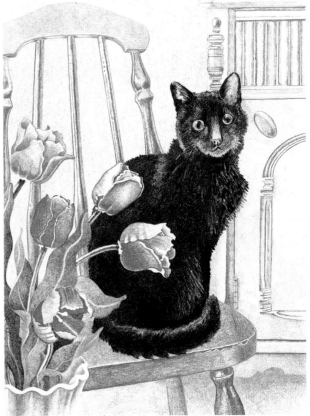

At this stage, the forms and color have been established with one layer on a medium-grained paper similar to that used for the original drawing. In some cases a color or value is incomplete because its completion will depend on a second layer. In the cabinet and flowers, the pencil colors used cannot deliver dark enough values, so these will be firmed up later by alayeral means.

Applying all the first layers of color before moving on to the second layers, as is done here, is a somewhat structured way of drawing. A more common method is the immediate layering of colors as needed. But I think that isolating the layers will better illustrate the concept we are dealing with.

The cat now has both its layers, dark blue and red, and it begins to read as a very black cat. A second layer has been begun on the cabinet, and the background has its silver addition.

To reduce what seemed too purple a cast in the original drawing, the purple was applied lightly this time. If the purple cast were to be duplicated, the purple would have to be applied heavily enough to assert itself more strongly through the silver. Letting the background read as more neutral will, I think, increase the drawing's overall contrast.

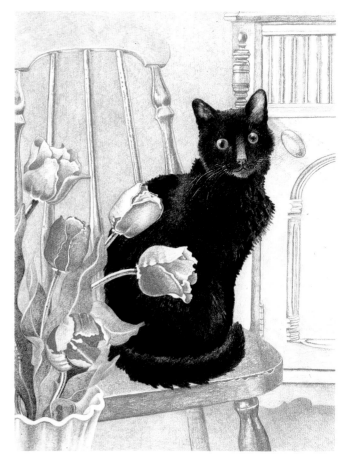

Adding light violet to the chair seems to help unify it with its surrounding negative space. The vase and flowers also have their second and final layers of color. If this were a new drawing, rather than a reconstruction, I would probably use a third layer on one or two of the flowers for a bit more color impact.

Except for the cabinet, the drawing has received all its color layers. At this point, close to the finish, it is time to assess its values and details and to make any planned adjustments.

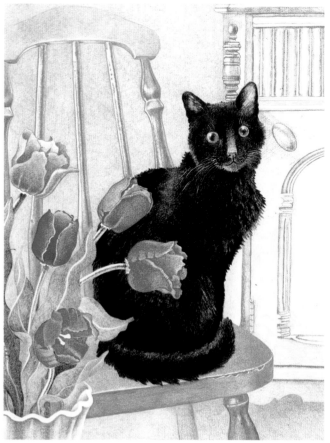

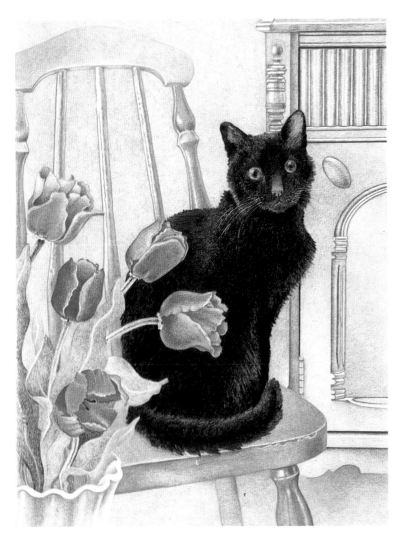

The second and final layer of color has been applied to the cabinet. Other adjustments to the drawing involved lightening some of the values of the cat, flowers, and chair seat with a kneaded eraser. Some values were darkened in the flowers and in the cabinet.

As you can see by comparing this drawing with its original version, two layers can accomplish a great deal in color mixing and complexity. The main drawback of this rigorous an approach is that color cannot be as easily and freely modulated as may be desired. In the section that follows, spot-layering will be explored as a fast-working answer to this.

What is Alayeral?

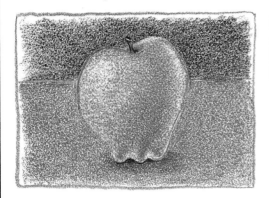

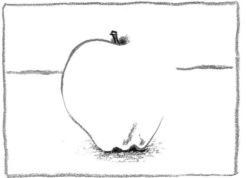

The alayeral parts of a color drawing are those that relate more to drawing itself than to color or layering. This includes all the strokes, blips, hits, and other marks that are critical to crisping an edge, darkening a value, or adding a line but are not layers, that is, have no direct function in color mixing.

The apple sketched at left contains layered color as well as alayeral work. If we could magically remove all the layered and mixed color to reveal only what is alayeral, our apple would look like the sketch at right.

4
SPOT-LAYERING

The idea behind spot-layering is to use small fragments or bits of color to further modulate a colored passage. You can save a great deal of drawing time by using these selective "spots" of color rather than more extensive layers. This technique works wonderfully well with the already time-saving two-layer approach to colored pencil drawing.

While a two-layer approach permits variations in mixture proportion, in value, and in intensity, it is not well suited to color modulation. And it is in color modulation that spot-layering—whether applied as a bold accent or feathered subtly into an area—comes to the rescue.

Spot-layering is most effective when it also re-lates to a firm understanding of what is alayeral (the barest strokes of drawing, but not of color) about our work. The connection here is that seeing alayerally can prepare us for thinking of color itself as a constantly merging and overlapping thing, rather than as applications of formal layers.

As we learn to think of our work in its separate parts—the alayeral, the limited layering, the spot-layering—the process of drawing with colored pencils speeds up dramatically. The bonus in quality this may also bring derives from a new ability to see color not as static mixtures but rather as the dynamic facets of true light's constant changes.

BEAUTY
Colored pencil on two-ply Strathmore bristol board, 17½" × 12¼" (44.5 cm × 31.1 cm). Collection of L'Ermitage Hotel, Beverly Hills, California.

In this drawing no more than two layers (and often only one layer) of pencil color were used anywhere. Spot-layering was used freely, as can be seen in the window sash, wallpaper, and dog.

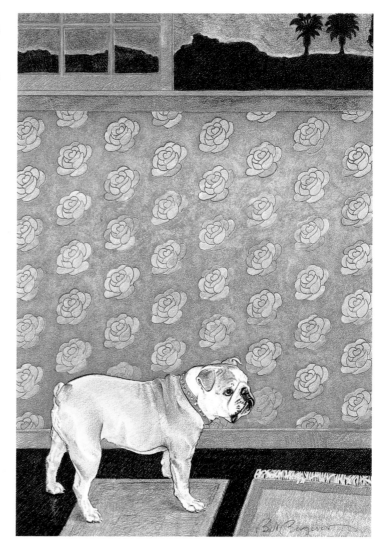

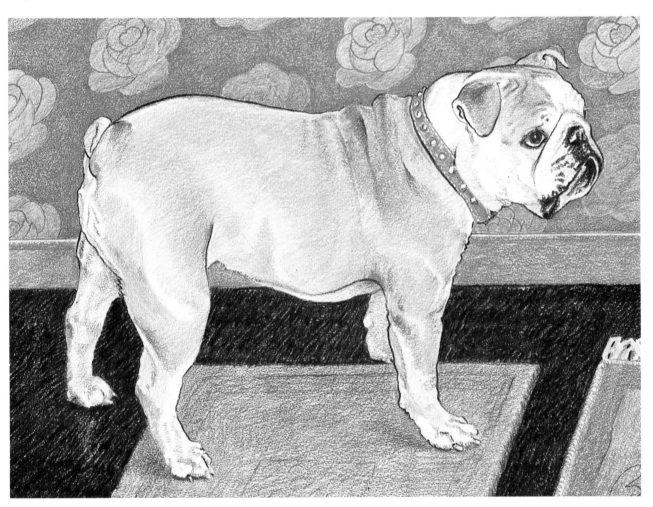

In the upper right section of wallpaper, spot-layering was used with little concern for finesse. It is a fast way of increasing color modulation, and in this case it also offered me an opportunity to restate the animal's boldness of spirit.

The detail below from the same drawing shows a more reserved use of spot-layering to model the dog's form. While the dog was rendered in only one layer of color, I used different pencils to produce that layer. The spot-layered color changes are not as distinct here as in the wallpaper, nor are their edges as visible.

Examples of Spot-Layering

These three small reconstructions from a colored pencil drawing show how spot-layering was used to quickly develop color.

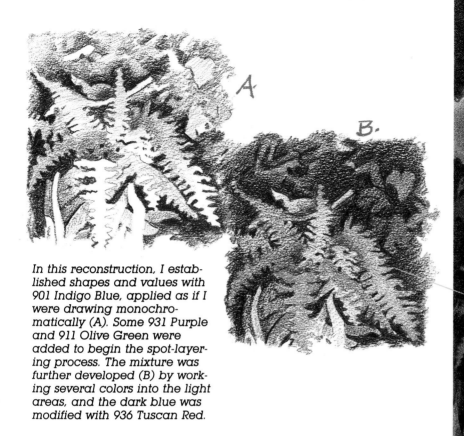

In this reconstruction, I established shapes and values with 901 Indigo Blue, applied as if I were drawing monochromatically (A). Some 931 Purple and 911 Olive Green were added to begin the spot-layering process. The mixture was further developed (B) by working several colors into the light areas, and the dark blue was modified with 936 Tuscan Red.

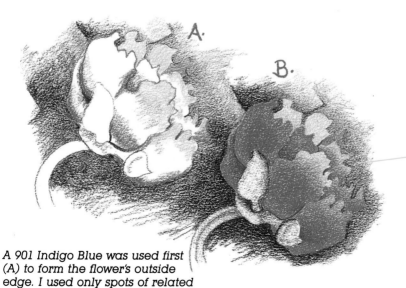

A 901 Indigo Blue was used first (A) to form the flower's outside edge. I used only spots of related color in the flower's interior, as a start toward modeling its form. These areas were then blended together (B) with still another related color.

SANCTUARY
Colored pencil on three-ply Strathmore bristol board, 18" × 25" (45.7 cm × 63.5 cm). Collection of L'Ermitage Hotel, Beverly Hills, California.

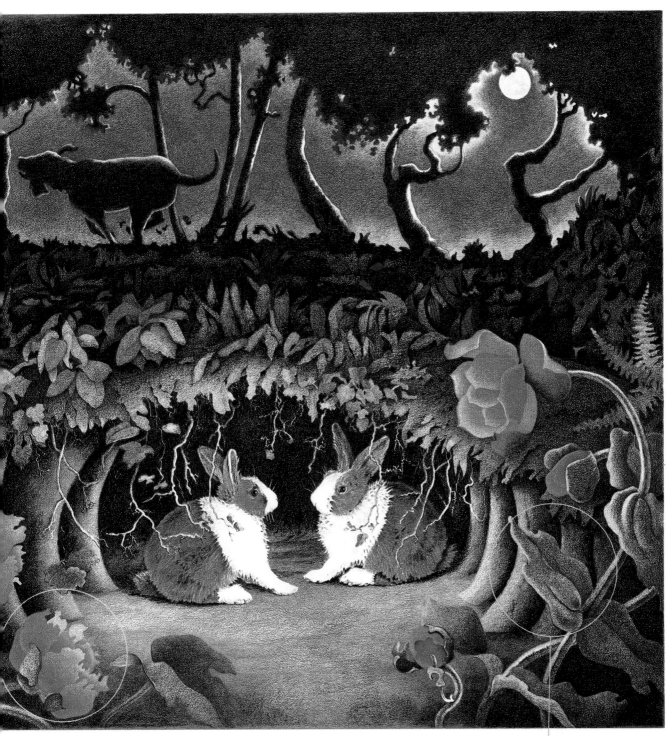

This example, like the others, shows how I used several colors that were not layered over one another but instead were spotted into selected areas, as in the leaf (A). These spots were then knitted together or blended with other colors (B).

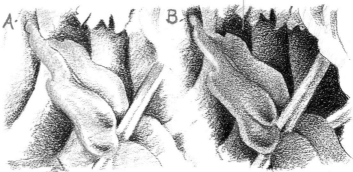

Step-By-Step
BOLD SPOT-LAYERING

Spot-layering can be bold or subtle, depending on your personal style and the needs of the work itself. In this drawing of a bird of paradise flower, my idea was to use color quickly and boldly to reinforce the plant's own dramatic nature.

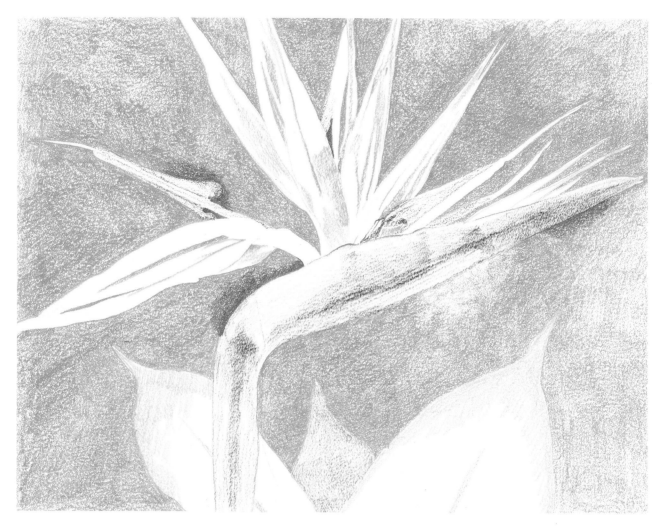

Step One. *I established my composition with an HB graphite pencil on two-ply Pacifica museum board (a fast-working surface). Then I tonally applied a layer of 993 Hot Pink to the negative space, working the pencil in all directions. Next, colors were spot-layered onto the flower—917 Yellow Orange, 918 Orange, and 903 True Blue on the "tongues." I used 909 Grass Green to begin modeling the form of the "boat." A 917 Yellow Orange pencil was used at the very tips of the leaves. A few spots of 932 Violet were added over the pink negative space to remind me of what the final mix here would be.*

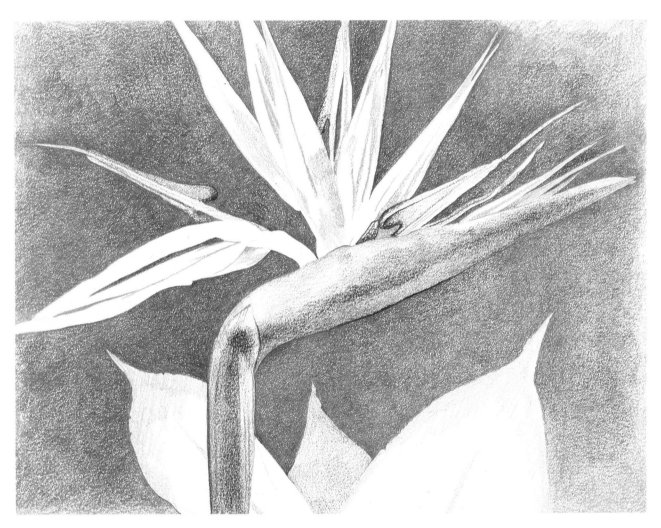

Step Two. The plant's "boat" was further modeled with 911 Olive Green. Some 934 Lavender and 903 True Blue were added to approximate the flower's actual local color, and 902 Ultramarine and 910 True Green were added to the blue "tongues." But the most important change was made in the negative space: I vigorously applied a 932 Violet pencil over the pink, allowing much of the original color to show through. I also added some 924 Crimson Red and 903 True Blue, instead of more violet, in selected areas of the background. These bold bursts of color will perform an important function in the next step.

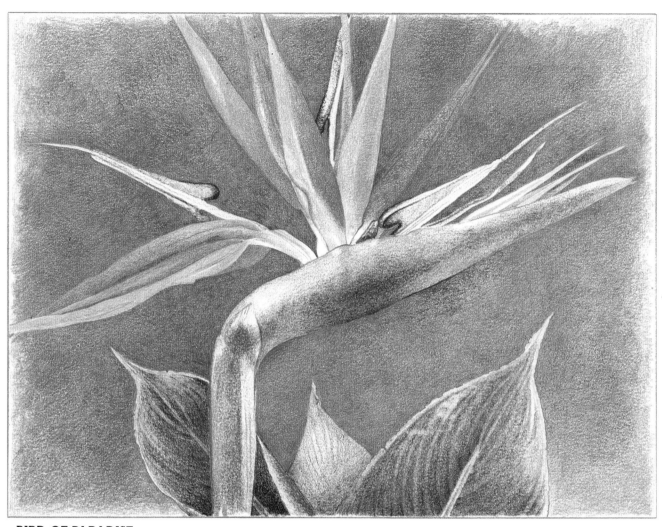

BIRD OF PARADISE
Colored pencil on Pacifica museum board, 7½″ × 10″ (19.1 cm × 25.4 cm). Private collection.

Step Three. *To finish the drawing, the "tongues" were completed with blended spot-layers of 918 Orange, 923 Scarlet Lake, 993 Hot Pink, and 924 Crimson Red. The "boat" was completed by returning to the original green (909 Grass Green) and blending patches of color together to restate the modeling more emphatically. The leaves were also completed with the same colors used for the "boat," plus some 901 Indigo Blue for a good dark value. Finally, the bursts of color spot-layered into the negative space were better integrated with the surrounding violet. Because they remain bold and separate, rather than being completely blended, they echo the color in the flower itself. This in turn helps the negative space appear atmospheric, making it seem to envelop the flower somewhat instead of lying flat behind it.*

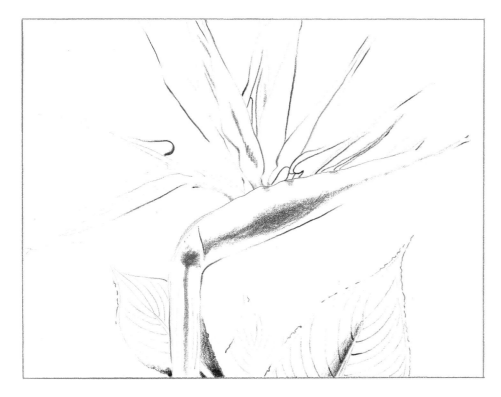

*If we could somehow re-
move all the layered
color from Bird of Para-
dise, here is how an
alayeral version of it
would look.*

*This shows both alayeral
work and spot-layering.
The overall layers and
the blending layers used
to join patches of color
have been omitted, but a
feeling of modulated
color can already be
seen in this lively sub-
structure.*

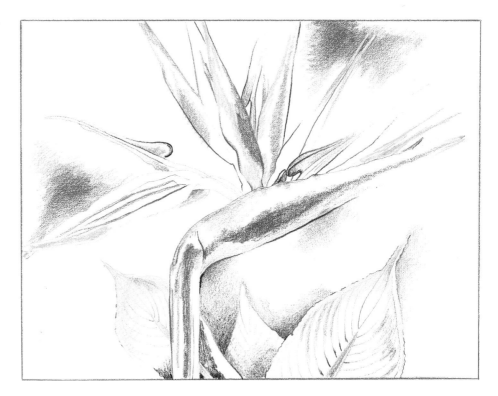

Step-By-Step
BLENDED SPOT-LAYERING

For a portrait to appear credible and lifelike, its flesh colors must be well modulated. This quality can be achieved with only two layers of pencil color when they are combined with blended spot-layering. In this informal portrait, spot-layering was used to represent the planes of the face and to suggest the model's own coloring.

Step One. The gestures of head and hair were first established with a spare graphite line on tracing paper. I begin this way because searching for form and the position and proportion of facial features usually includes false starts, and I would rather make erasures on tracing paper than on my final drawing surface. My guidelines were then lightly transferred to a sheet of Stonehenge paper. A soft surface such as Stonehenge is a good choice for colored pencil portraiture, because the subtle blending of flesh colors can be rapidly achieved on it with only light-to-medium pencil pressure.

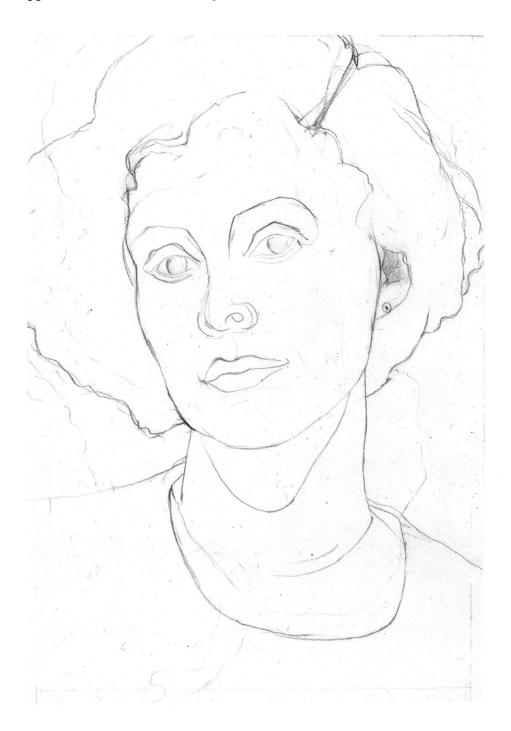

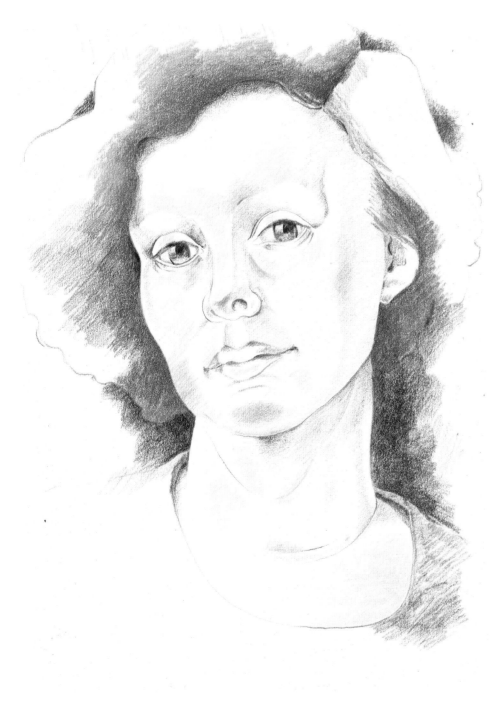

Step Two. *Spot-layers of color have been laid in but not blended. The colors of the large areas—hair, background, and blouse—were brought in as an environment or surrounding to help with hue and value decisions in the face. These areas don't require much pigment yet, but the colors must be in close proximity to the facial features. Small bits of color—942 Yellow Ochre, 923 Scarlet Lake, 929 Pink, 910 True Green, and 918 Orange—were laid in to begin mixing flesh colors and modeling features. A 932 Violet, used for the head's core shadow, will later be mixed with 931 Purple.*

Step Three. Ordinarily, each spot-layered color would be blended immediately as drawing progressed alla prima, or all at once. The spot-layers have been held back from such mixing to show them more clearly. A 939 Flesh was the pencil used most to knit colors together, but the spot-layering colors were sometimes used to smooth transitions. The violet of the core shadows—used to signal plane changes—was mixed with a 931 Purple. I didn't use the violet alone because it tends to appear hazy and insubstantial by itself, and it wouldn't suggest the solidity I was looking for.

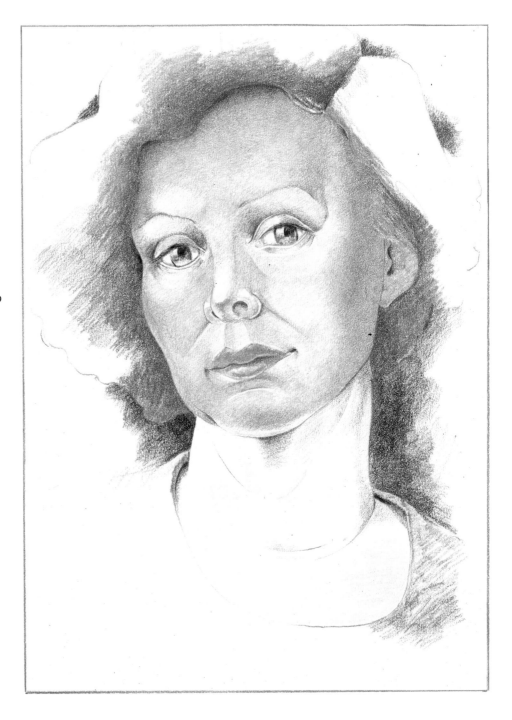

KATE
Colored pencil on Stonehenge paper, 11″ × 7″ (27.9 cm × 17.8 cm). Private collection.

I completed the hair and blouse first so I could better assess what other adjustments seemed necessary. The neck was developed further with the same palette used for the face, to which I added a 906 Copenhagen Blue. This cool color was used to help place the neck securely back under the head. Finally, a few last alayeral adjustments were made. These included darkening the color of the upper eyelids and firming the modeling along the outside contours of the neck and cheeks.

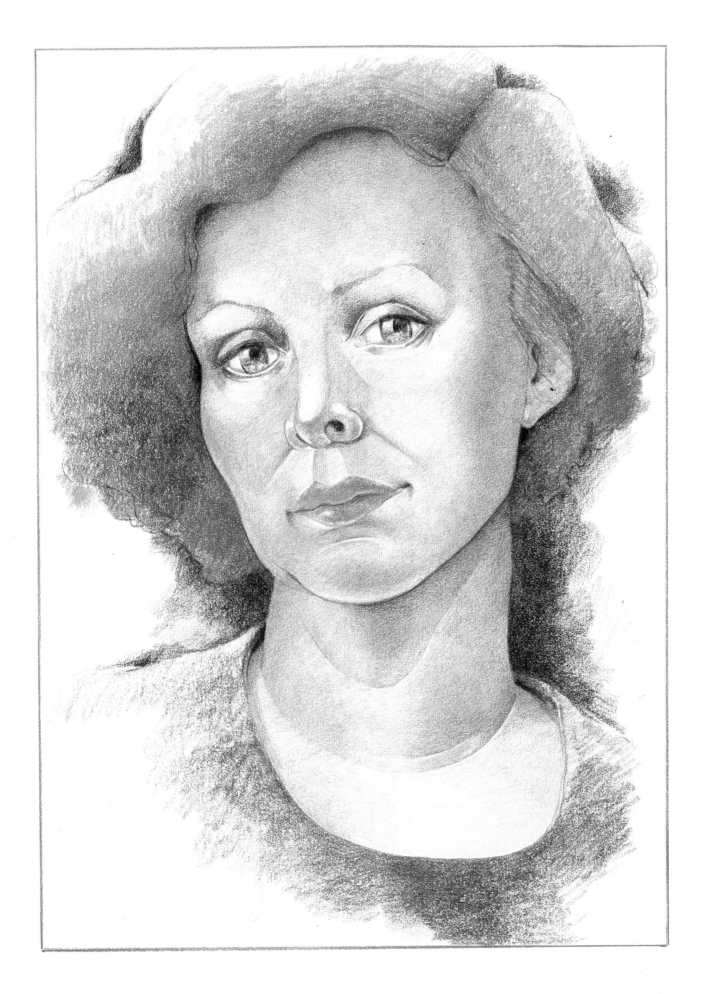

JUXTAPOSING COLOR

Juxtaposing color, for our purposes, means arranging areas of color side by side rather than overlaying them. These juxtaposed areas can be mere strokes or larger passages of color. This technique can be a way of achieving color complexity in less time than with layering.

The fastest way to get juxtaposed color results is with single layers, but this kind of mixing also works well with a two-layer approach. Among the possible two-layer arrangements are:

1. First layer a single color; second layer juxtaposed colors.

2. First layer juxtaposed colors; second layer a single color.

3. First layer juxtaposed colors; second layer juxtaposed colors.

Two or more colors can be used in this side-by-side way, and a single juxtaposed layer may include a number of separate colors that are all somehow related to one another. Reasons for choosing to group certain colors are of course purely personal, but the basic relationships among most color groupings tend to be:

1. Analogous colors

2. Complementary or near-complementary colors

3. All bright colors

4. All dull colors

5. Colors of contrasting temperature (warm-cool-warm)

Much time can be saved by juxtaposing colors as mixtures. But there is an even more important additional benefit to be gained from learning to see and use color in this way: It further promotes an ability to differentiate colors in groupings of seemingly identical objects, whether a bunch of bananas or a field of flowers.

Juxtaposed colors can be used in situations ranging from close detail to broad sweeps. All these sketches (A through D) were made with analogous colors applied side by side.

Within the single petal (A), three colors—917 Yellow Orange, 923 Scarlet Lake, and 925 Crimson Lake—are juxtaposed side by side. In the group of petals (B), the same three colors were used, plus 924 Crimson Red and 922 Scarlet Red. But this time each petal is a different color, and the petals themselves do the juxtaposing. In the two individual flowers (C), a single pencil was used for each (except for a few alayeral details); the juxtaposition of color happens from flower to flower. With the field of flowers (D), all the red through yellow-orange colors are juxtaposed rather than layered, resulting in an optical rather than a physical mixture.

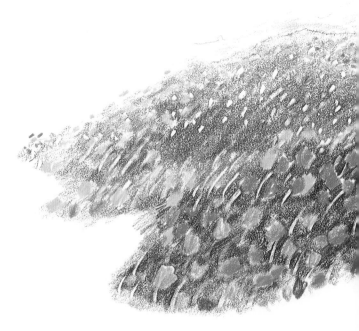

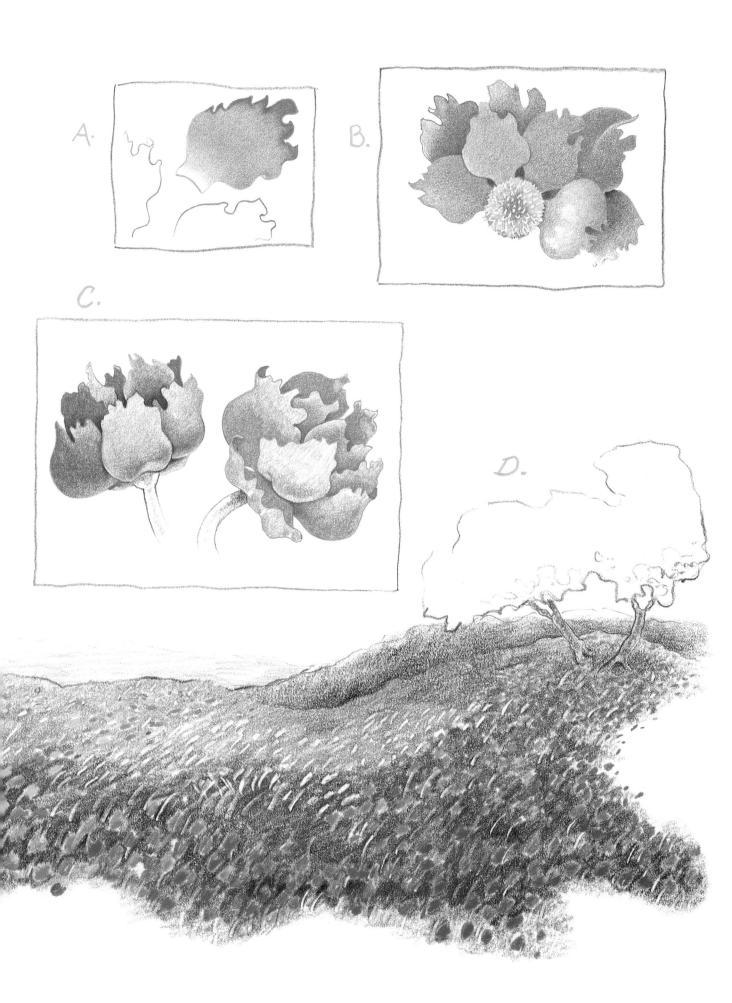

Using Interacting Colors

Color expressed with a lone colored pencil often appears raw and simplistic. To overcome this drawback of single-pencil layering— while retaining the advantage of its speed—a more complex layer can be created by juxtaposing colors that are related or that interact with one another in some way. Here are a few of the ways in which juxtaposed colors can interact.

Analogous. Analogous colors are similar to one another; the term usually refers to adjacent colors on a color wheel. Colored pencils often contain many variations within a hue family, so similar might also refer to colors of the same hue, such as all the reds or all the greens.

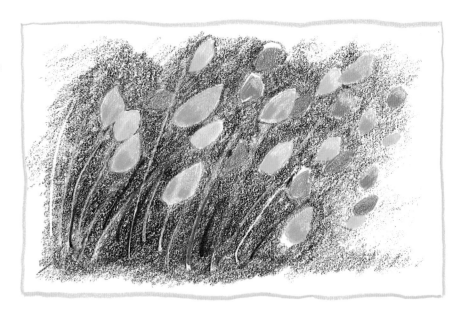

Complementary. Complementary colors are opposite one another on the color wheel. In practice, we usually deal with near-complementary or nearly opposite colors. Here, the field is a single blue, and the spots are drawn with various orange and yellow-orange pencils.

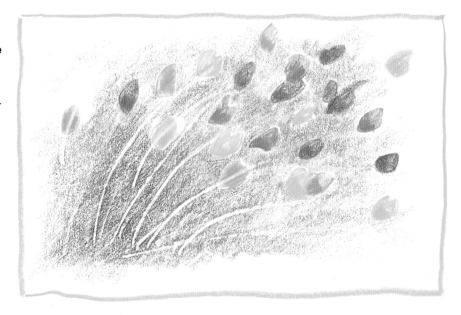

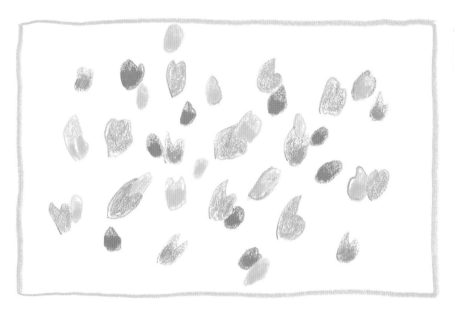

All Bright Colors. In this example, the brilliant white of the paper itself contributes to the "all bright" scheme.

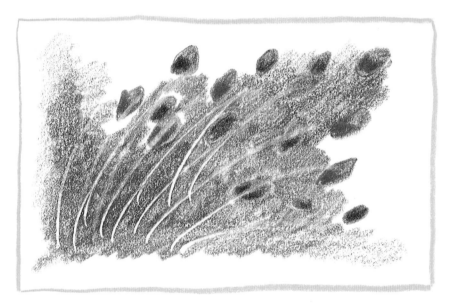

All Dull Colors. The word "dull" is not a pejorative in the case of colors; it merely refers to colors of low intensity.

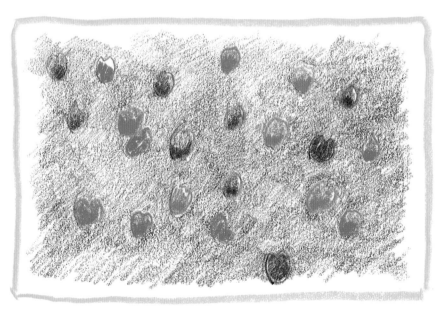

Colors of Contrasting Temperatures. Temperatures of colors may vary depending on their environments. For this reason, temperature was not included in the Hue-Value-Intensity Charts in the Appendix. A color's temperature is best assessed in the context of the other colors that you plan to use near it.

Examples of Juxtaposed Color

This drawing contains very little layering. Where layering does occur, it was done in almost every case with a scant spot-layering technique. Most of the color mixing depends instead on the juxtaposition of colors. It is in fact just such a pictorial situation as this—with extensive repetition of similar objects such as the tree leaves—that invites a strategy of quickly juxtaposing colors rather than attempting to layer them.

A scheme of three simple analogous colors plus white was used for the tree foliage (A). In the small reconstruction (B), the red-orange wood and the foliage can be seen juxtaposed in a near-complementary color scheme. Most of the colors are single layers, but occasionally a previously applied color was adjusted with another one.

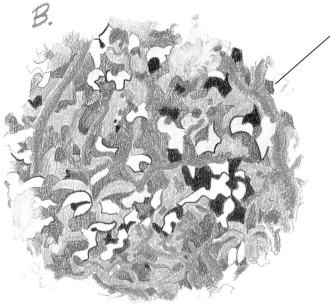

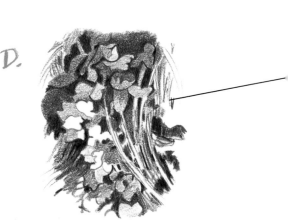

The scheme for the little floral detail was made up of three analogous pencil colors, plus a linear accent of scarlet lake (C). In the reconstruction (D), the dark value of the background was also included. Conventional layering was completely bypassed in this passage. Instead, various values of analogous colors were used to suggest the facet-like shapes of the flowers.

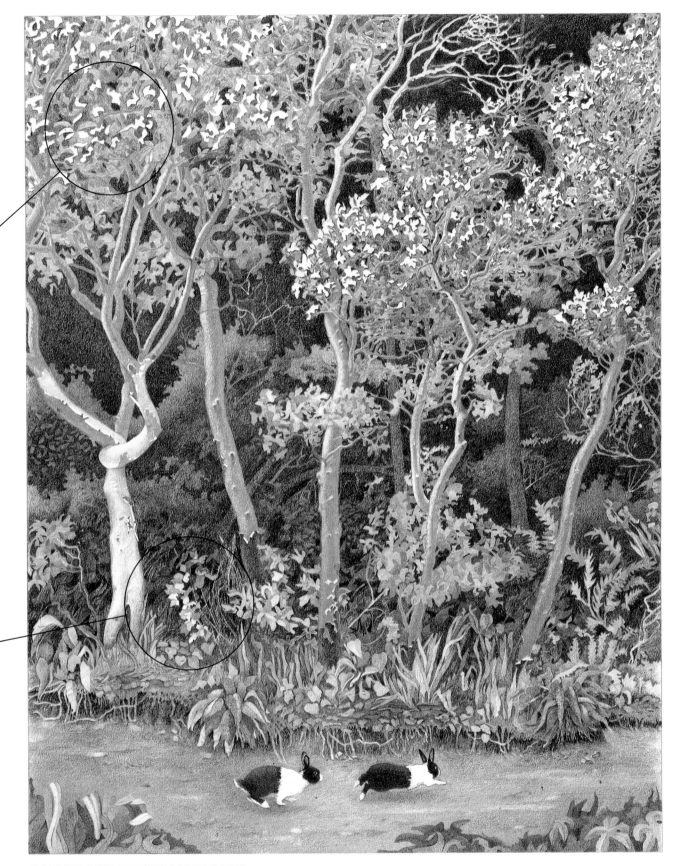

RABBITS AND YOUNG MADRONES
Colored pencil on three-ply Strathmore bristol board, 25½″ × 20″ (64.8 cm × 50.8 cm).
Collection of Mr. and Mrs. John Loewen, Portland, Oregon.

Step-By-Step
JUXTAPOSED COLOR

Juxtaposed color can not only be quickly used to mix and suggest local color, but can also be used as an effective and simple way to achieve depth.

Step One. *After lightly laying in graphite guidelines, I started drawing the floor with two juxtaposed colors. The cooler of these two colors, a 923 Scarlet Lake, was used toward the back to begin establishing depth, and a warmer 922 Scarlet Red was used at the front. Although the floor was done quite swiftly, care was taken to join the colors invisibly. The cat—the only element for which three color layers were planned—was begun with a 901 Indigo Blue.*

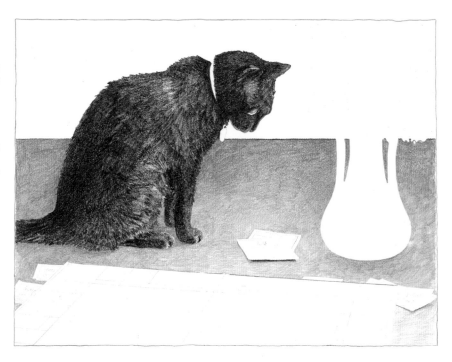

Step Two. *The molding and plant leaves were begun with analogous colors, 903 True Blue and 905 Aquamarine. The wall was loosely established with a 918 Orange and the flowers with 923 Scarlet Lake. Undersides of the flower petals were drawn by juxtaposing 931 Purple, 934 Lavender, and 956 Light Violet petal to petal. The cat was modified with a second layer of 937 Tuscan Red, and the game board was also begun.*

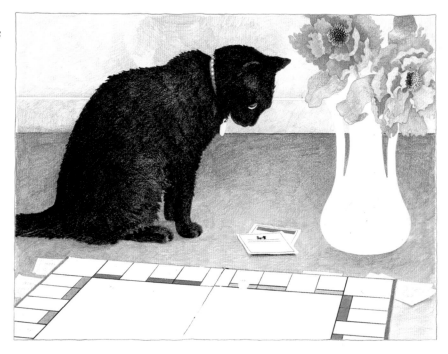

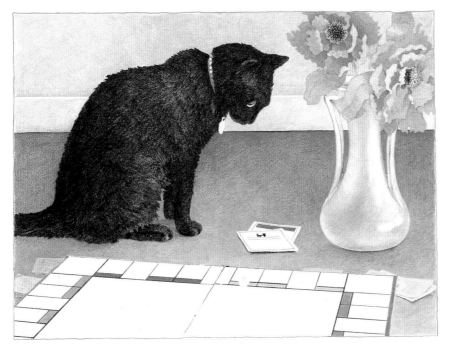

Step Three. As a final layer of juxtaposed color for the floor, a 931 Purple was used at the back, blended into a bright 917 Yellow Orange at the front. This same warm yellow-orange was also spot-layered into the wall, the molding, and the flower petals. The undersides of the petals were not changed. The vase was modeled in a mostly alayeral fashion, with various light tints of color.

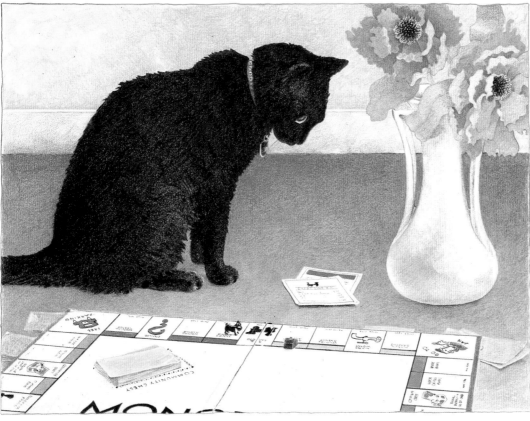

QUIET GAME
Colored pencil on four-ply Rising museum board, 12″ × 16″ (30.5 cm × 40.6 cm). Collection of L'Ermitage Hotel, Beverly Hills, California.

Step Four. To complete the drawing, a final layer of 931 Purple was applied to the cat and details were added to the game board. Several alayeral adjustments—almost always needed at this point—were made. Values were darkened where appropriate with colored pencil or lightened with a kneaded eraser. Except for the cat, which was drawn with three layers, none of this drawing's elements contains more than one or two layers, and all the layers were applied with spot-layering or juxtaposed color techniques.

6

USING LINE WITH TONE

Purely linear drawing is the fastest technique with any pencil, colored or graphite, and it works particularly well with graphite. But with colored pencils, the mixing of colors is all but imperative, and line alone is seldom enough.

There are many opportunities in colored pencil work to profit from line's superior speed. Usually this is done by combining line with tone, which can impart a vigorous texture to otherwise static tonal passages.

The uses of line with tone may be extensive or very spare; this is a matter of personal choice and must be consistent with one's own style. Other ways to incorporate line include using it to abut tonal passages, as in the handling of outside contour edges.

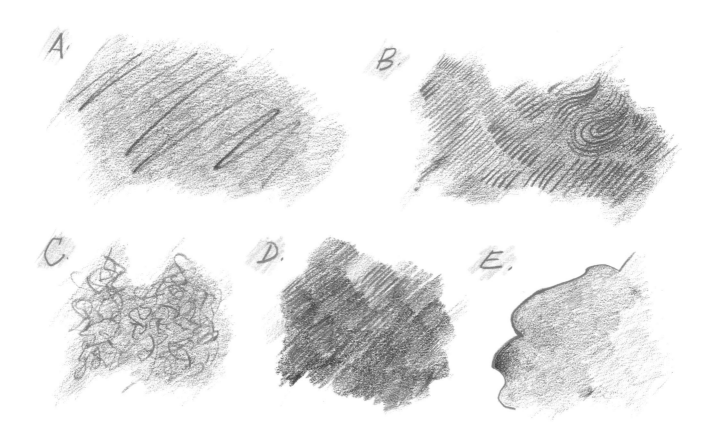

Here are just a few of the numerous ways in which line can work well with tone:

A. A loose, open line cutting across a tone.

B. A controlled line or hatching. The color of the hatching lines can be changed as needed.

C. A personal kind of stroke—in this case, an eccentric calligraphic line.

D. Tone applied over line.

E. A line constructed of two separate colors abutting a tonal area.

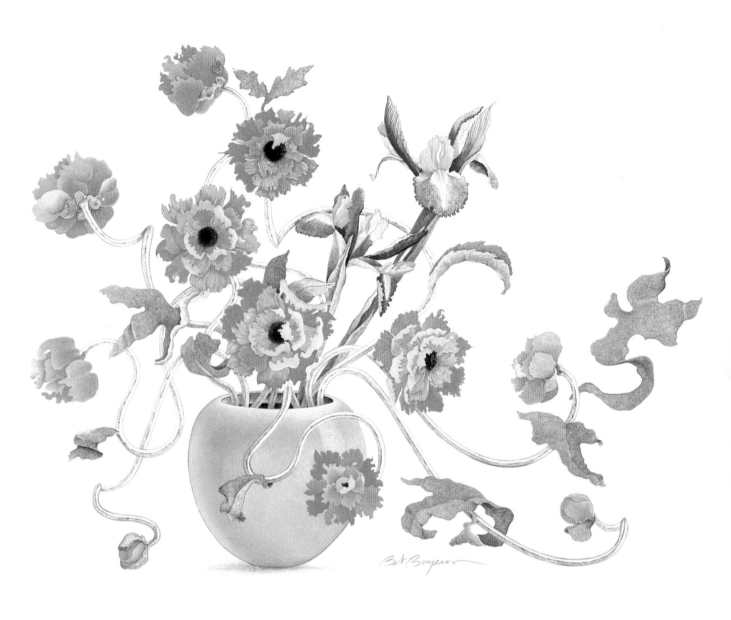

WHITE FLORAL #2
Colored pencil on four-ply Rising museum board, 31″ × 38″ (78.7 cm × 96.5 cm). Private collection.

Line was used in two ways in this drawing; the most immediately visible linear work is that in the flower petals. The color mixing here was based on a simple juxtaposition of analogous reds and oranges. Adding line to the tone helps make the petals appear richly contoured and textured.

A more subtle use of line can be seen on the outside contour edges of some of the leaves. This was done to provide a note of hue contrast to what is otherwise only an uncomplicated green.

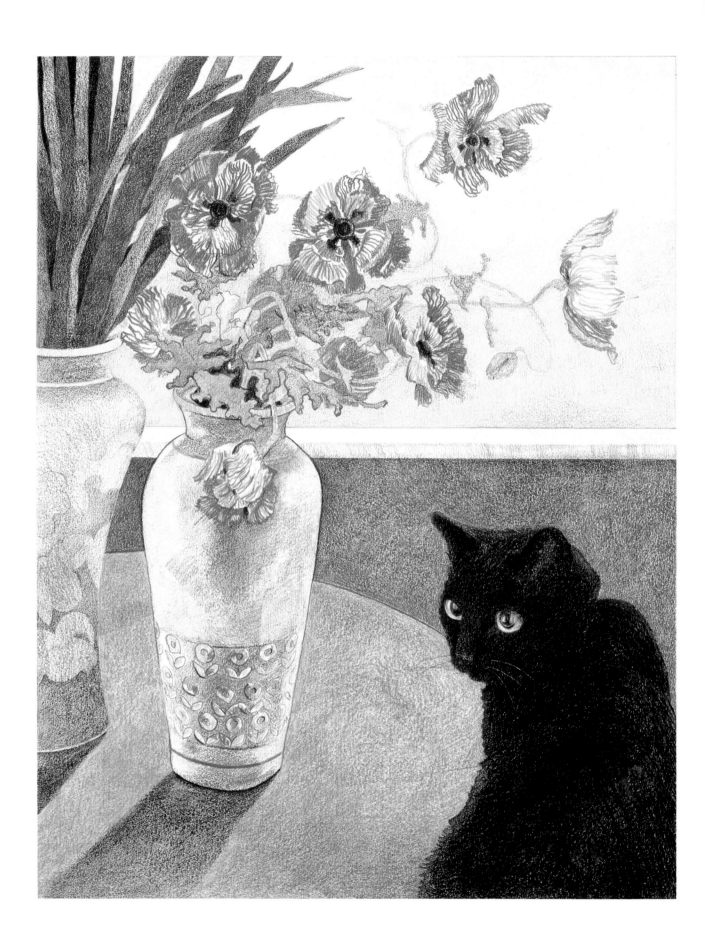

FASTER WAYS OF WORKING TO EDGES

By its nature, drawing with a sharpened pencil—graphite or colored—appeals particularly to the artist who prefers a clear, crisp delineation of form. To this end, a great deal of time is quietly spent constructing edges where the shapes or contours of elements come together. With colored pencils, however, there are several faster ways than those traditionally employed for working to edges.

These methods are not "shortcuts" in the sense that they lessen quality; rather, they seize the opportunities offered by the colored pencil medium itself. The fact is, colored pencil edges that are made with increased speed can almost always duplicate the character of slower-made edges. And by avoiding the drastic slowdown that often accompanies the handling of edges, faster-made edges can also preserve much vital creative momentum.

Of course, some areas of edges will continue to require acute concentration and extra time. But for those areas where the medium favors greater speed, it is simply a matter of matching up colored pencil techniques with the appropriate edge situations.

CAT AND POPPIES
Colored pencil on two-ply Strathmore bristol board,
14" × 11" (35.6 cm × 27.9 cm). Private collection.

A variety of edge qualities can be seen in this drawing: blurred, hard, linear, high contrast, and low contrast. This is not unusual in a drawing or painting, and it affords many opportunities for using a variety of fast-working edge techniques.

Using Graphite for Edges

Graphite pencils are frequently used to establish guidelines, which are then erased as the color work proceeds. This time-consuming erasure step is generally unnecessary, except when very light-colored passages are being developed. Think of graphite as simply a color of very low intensity, for in practice it often acts like a chameleon, blending invisibly into its surrounding environment.

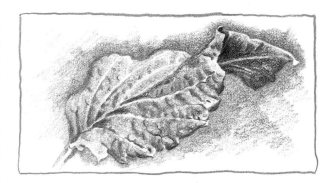

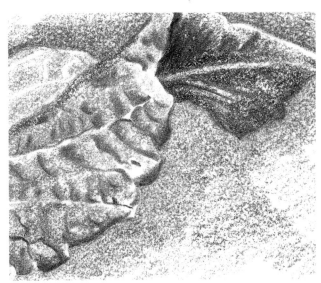

The graphite edge is virtually invisible in this drawing of a leaf (top), even though it has not been erased or even lightened. A closer view (bottom) shows the graphite is still barely visible; it has either blended with the green or been hidden by it.

Using a Darker Pencil First

When working to an edge with two layers of color, try laying in the darker color first. Use this pencil to carefully describe the edge. The second layer, made with the less conspicuous lighter pencil, can then be applied fairly casually, letting this layer only approximately (rather than precisely) meet the edge. You will find that edges fashioned in this way look no different from slowly drawn edges, but you will have had to work slowly and precisely only once instead of twice.

In this small design, 932 Violet was used as the first layer. Because it is the darker of the two colors planned for the area, the violet was used to carefully delineate the edge.

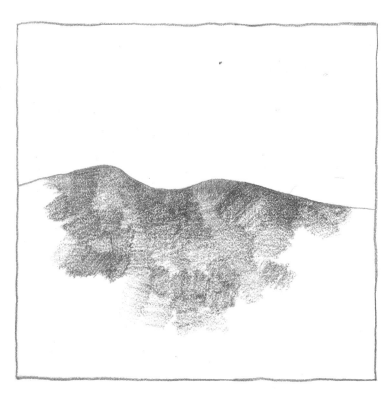

The second layer, 903 True Blue, was then applied. Because it is lighter than the original violet, there was no need to slow down this time. Sometimes the blue touches the edge, sometimes it doesn't—but the imprecision does not appear to be a problem.

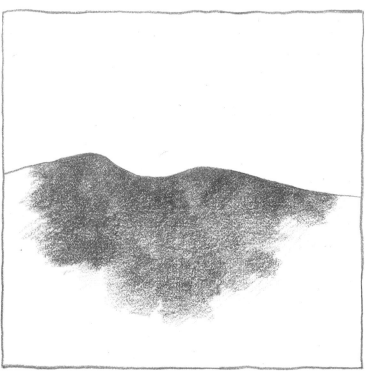

Letting Colors Spill Over Edges

Another time-saver with edges is allowing light colors to spill over into darker surrounds. Lighter colors influence dark passages only very slightly, if at all, and even when light colors do spill over, the resulting edge can look as crisp as one that took twice as long to draw. This technique can sometimes be used with colors that are close in value if they are also similar in hue.

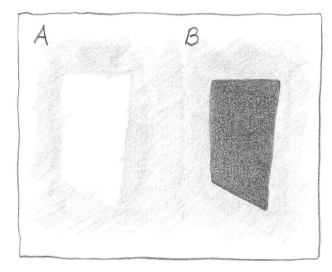

The first rectangle (A) was shaped by quickly—and less than precisely—laying in the light color of the negative space. In the finished rectangle (B), the more carefully applied darker color easily conceals the lighter color that spilled into that area. This would have worked equally well had the order of application been reversed.

In the second rectangle (C), a darker color has been used for the negative space; it has been applied imprecisely. The completed rectangle (D) was drawn with a color similar in both hue and value to the background. Again, the edge imperfections are masked.

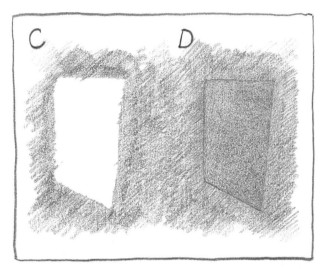

Avoiding Haloes

Gains in speed may also lead to improvements in edge quality. One reason: Just giving more consideration to how shapes are joined can improve edge character. A more important reason: Trying too hard to stay within lines— a kind of coloring-book approach—often results in tiny unintentional rims of light between shapes. Such a halo effect is shown in the small design at right. The cure for edge halo is using the edge techniques discussed and adopting a more relaxed attitude about drawing across edges.

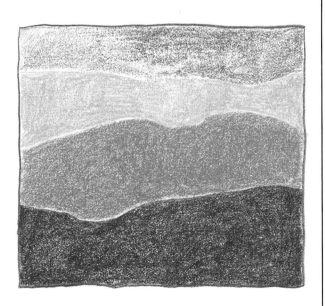

Working to a Linear Edge

When a colored line is to abut or surround an area of contrasting color, it is important that the line not be accidentally toned over and the purity of its color lost. To quickly preserve a very distinct line, colored lines can be impressed.

On Soft Surfaces

There is a simple way to draw lines that remain distinct even when surrounded by tonal work; this only works on soft surfaces, however. When you draw the linear details, use extra pressure to impress the line into the surface of the paper or board. Tonal strokes applied afterward will skip across the impressed colored lines, leaving them unchanged. This technique was used in *Blue Floral* (below), which was drawn on soft four-ply Rising museum board; the linear edges are visible on the spearlike leaves as well as on some of the lower leaves.

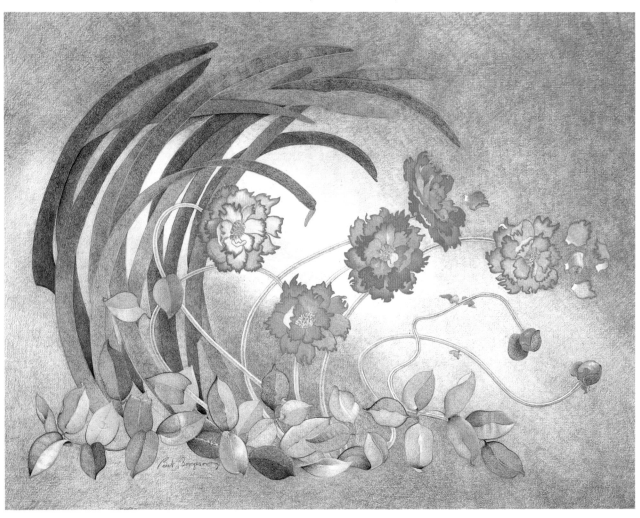

BLUE FLORAL
Colored pencil on four-ply Rising museum board, 25" × 33" (63.5 cm × 83.8 cm). Collection of L'Ermitage Hotel, Beverly Hills, California.

On Harder Surfaces

There are at least two situations in which colored linear edges cannot be preserved with heavier pencil pressure alone: The colored line may be of light value, and thus must be drawn with light pressure, or the working surface may be relatively hard. In both these cases, a colored line can be impressed with a tracing paper technique.

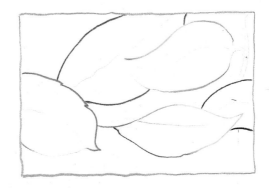

Imagine this small passage is part of a larger drawing. The tonal work will describe leaves, with some linear edges for hue contrast. Following light graphite guidelines, I drew the linear edges with various colored pencils, using medium pressure.

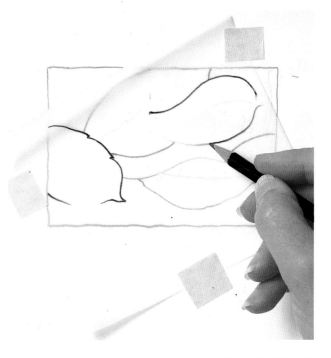

The area was then covered with a piece of tracing paper and, with an HB graphite pencil and firm pressure, I traced over the colored lines. The time you spend on this step will be more than regained as you proceed.

The tracing paper has been removed, and the process of applying tonal color to leaves and negative space has begun. Because my linear edges are now safely impressed below the paper's surface, the tonal work proceeds rapidly, crossing over colored lines with no danger of obscuring or losing them. This can be seen where the green has been applied over clearly visible red and yellow lines.

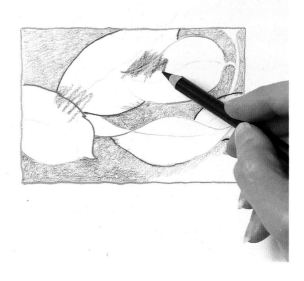

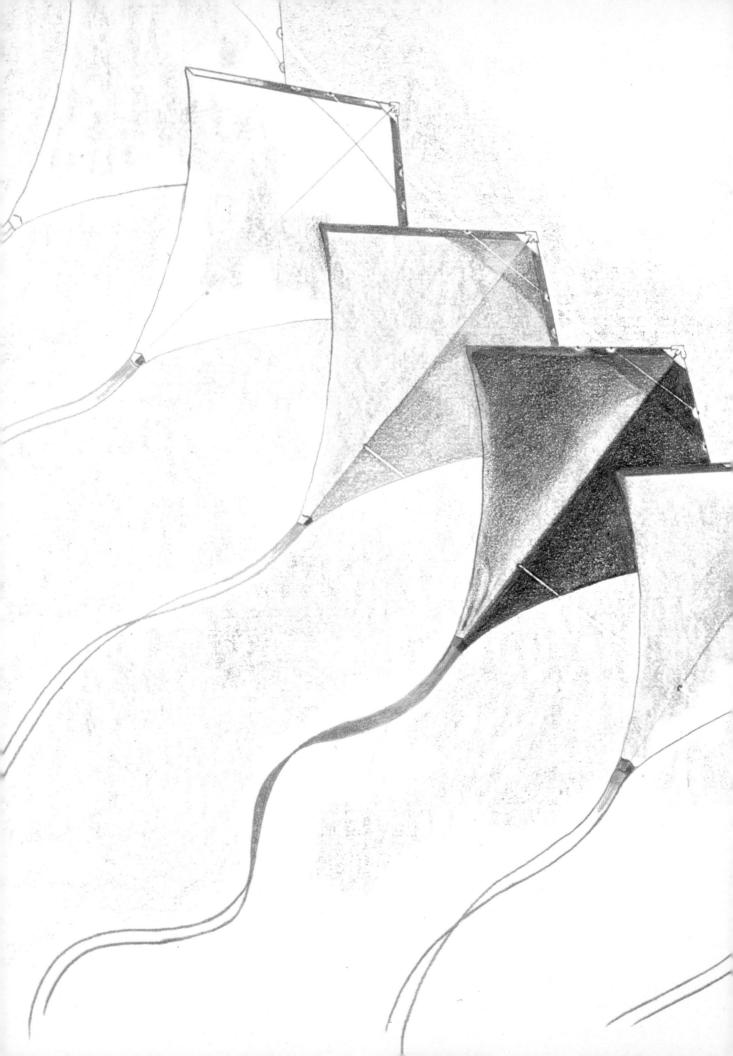

HANDLING BACKGROUNDS AND OTHER LARGE AREAS

The prospect of covering large surfaces with only the point of a pencil is undoubtedly the single most compelling reason why colored pencil work is often of small dimensions. In Part Two we will discuss a number of strategies and techniques related to eliminating this problem while at the same time creating rich and subtle color.

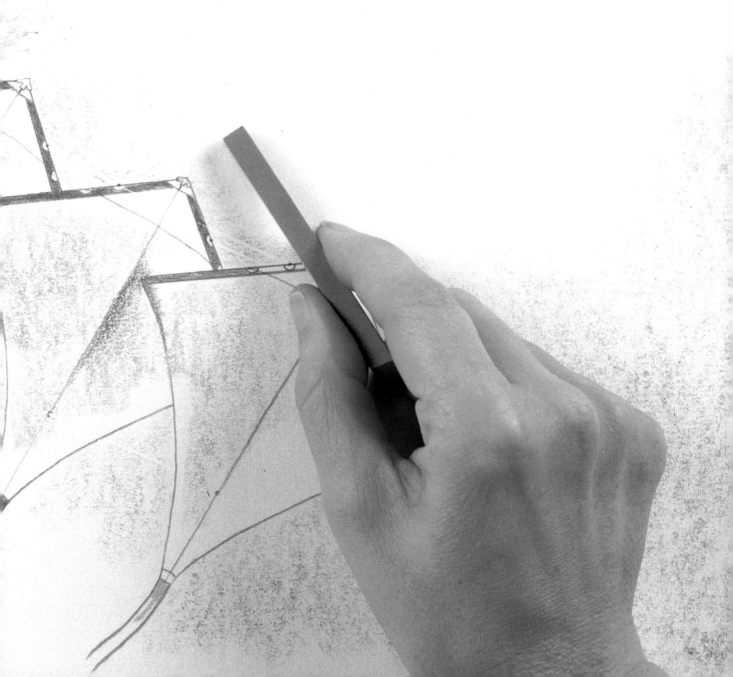

BEGINNING WITH BROAD STICK COLORS

In colored pencil, as in all pencil work, the handling of backgrounds and other large areas is always in danger of getting short shrift. Covering large areas of a surface with a small pencil point is a tedious task. One response to this is to apply backgrounds too hastily. Another is a hesitance to attempt work beyond small dimensions.

With colored pencils, however, there are some techniques and strategies that can drastically reduce the time needed to successfully handle large areas.

The simplest and most straightforward way of dealing with large and relatively simple areas is with the broad stick versions of colored pencil pigments now offered by some colored pencil makers. These sticks can be used to lay in a first application of color very rapidly. A sharpened colored pencil can then be used for those places where the stick is too large and to further smooth out the layer applied with the stick if necessary. It is a swift process and can of course be used for areas of positive as well as negative space.

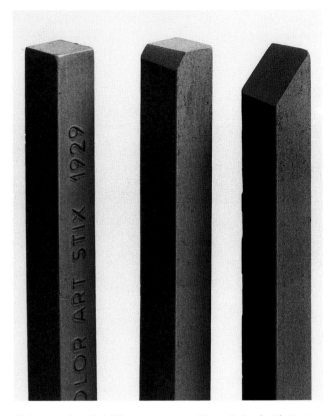

Prismacolor Art Stix are crayonlike sticks (left) that correspond in color to Prismacolor colored pencils. If you want to use them to cleanly deliver a flat application of color, first bevel the tip slightly (center). This flat bevel is made with a firm back-and-forth motion on a piece of scratch paper; hold the stick as it will be held for drawing and take care not to round its edges. The stick at right shows the more extreme bevel developed by contact with the drawing surface.

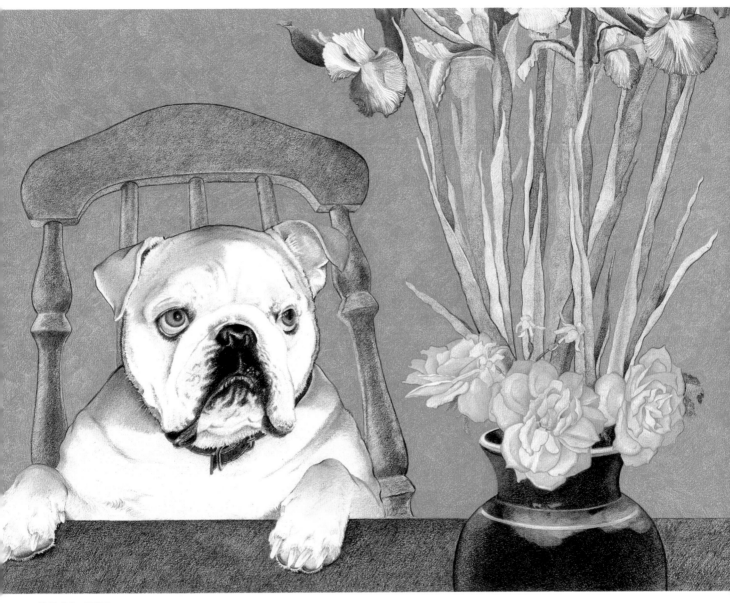

GOOD GIRL
Colored pencil on three-ply Strathmore bristol board, 17½" × 24½" (44.5 cm × 62.2 cm).
Private collection.

In this drawing, the colors of the background, the tabletop, and parts of the vase and chair were first laid down with Prismacolor Art Stix. Using these pigment sticks for a first layer often results in a texture that can be refined with a colored pencil or overridden by a new texture made with an added layer of colored pencil. The latter method was used in this drawing.

Step-By-Step
QUICKLY ESTABLISHING LARGE AREAS OF COLOR

The broad stick versions of colored pencils can be used for completed single layers or as first layers to be covered or modified later. They can also be superimposed on one another. Broad sticks will be used here as a means of delivering preliminary color to just the large areas of a drawing.

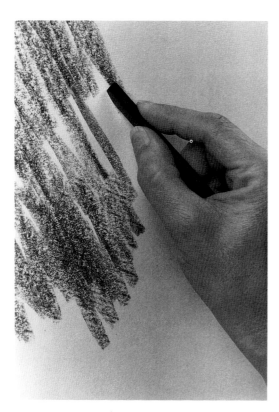

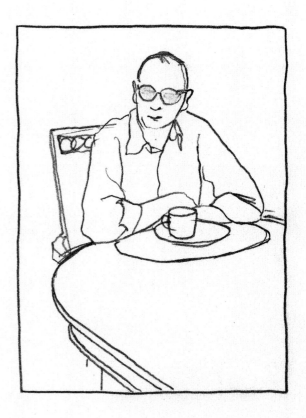

To deliver a consistent tone with a minimum of dark streaks, I hold the colored stick between thumb and fingers as shown and work standing at a near-vertical board. You will soon develop a grasp and method that are right for you. The important thing is that the stick's flat surface remain squarely on the bottom, against the paper surface. The stick is run back and forth in the area to be covered, with a motion similar to that of ironing fabric. Practice holding the stick's bevel flat, not letting it rock from side to side.

Thumbnail. This small preliminary sketch for a large drawing contains two areas that are both large and free of complexity: the table area and the background. It is in situations such as this that using broad color sticks can reduce color application time from hours to minutes.

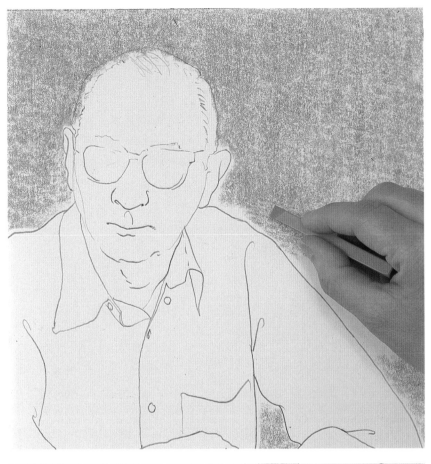

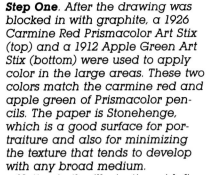

Step One. *After the drawing was blocked in with graphite, a 1926 Carmine Red Prismacolor Art Stix (top) and a 1912 Apple Green Art Stix (bottom) were used to apply color in the large areas. These two colors match the carmine red and apple green of Prismacolor pencils. The paper is Stonehenge, which is a good surface for portraiture and also for minimizing the texture that tends to develop with any broad medium.*

Notice in the illustration at left how the red runs over the line of the hair. Since the hair will be darker than the red background, the runover will not matter. The green at right, on the other hand, gives a wide berth to the placemat, which will be of a lighter color. The green will be brought to its final edge here with the point of a colored pencil.

For this drawing, I am keeping the values relatively unchanged. Values can be lightened or darkened somewhat with Art Stix, but when used flatly they don't have as wide a value range as the corresponding pencils.

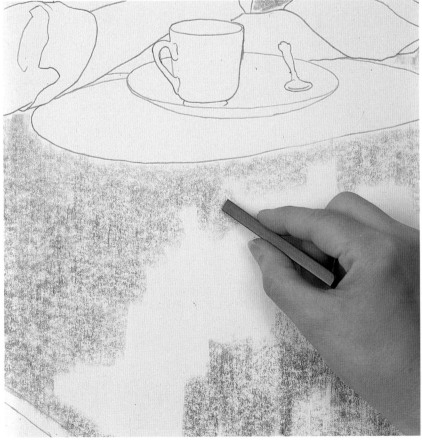

Step Two. Developing color with Art Stix is usually a two-step process. The stick is first used to quickly apply a layer of color, then a pencil is used to finish the layer.

In this case, I used corresponding pencil colors to refine the stick texture and to finish bringing color to some of the edges. I don't consider this pencil work a separate layer, but rather a smoothing out of any mottled or light/dark areas resulting from the stick.

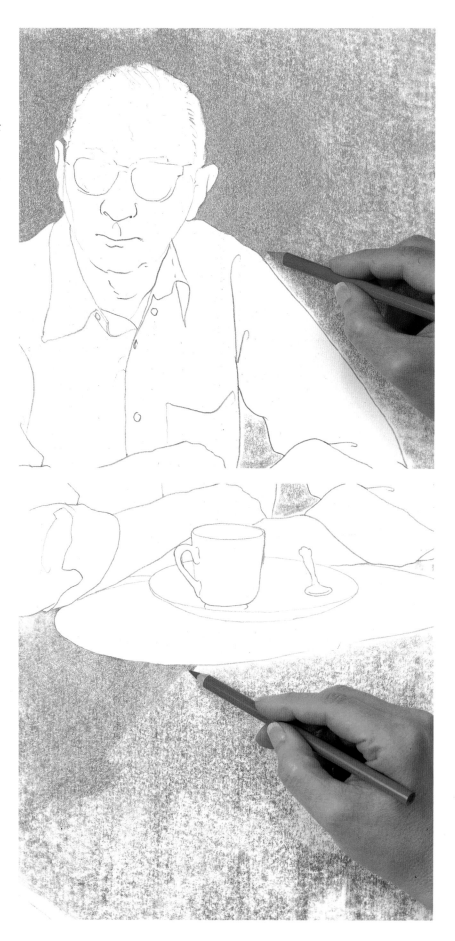

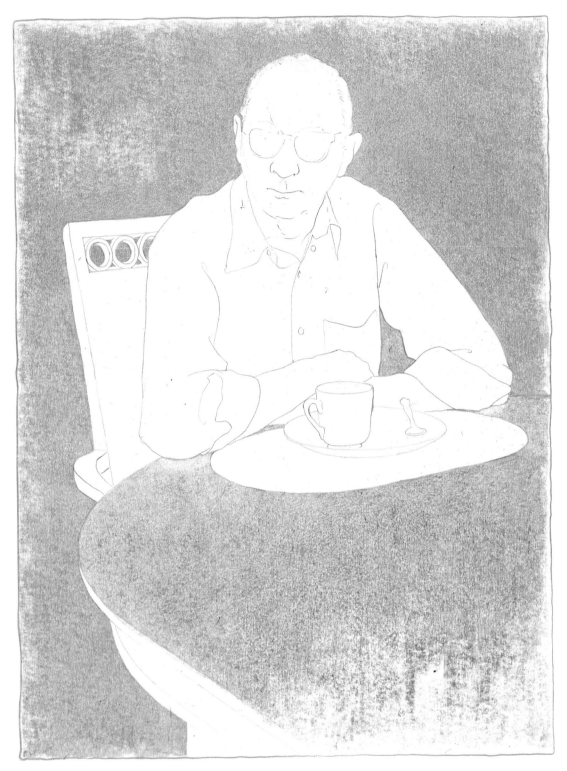

Here is how the entire background and table areas look at this stage. A first layer of Art Stix combined with corresponding Prismacolor pencils has been rapidly completed and is ready for any additional color work.

Note the texture. Where pencil color has been added, the surface is still nubby, but it appears refined compared with areas where no pencil was used, as in the lower right area of the table. Here the texture was deliberately allowed to show as a way of opening up the composition or relaxing the outside edges of the drawing. This area would probably not receive any more color. How much you should refine an Art Stix application—as with all color work—will finally depend on your personal aesthetics and needs.

Broad Stick Colors Combined with Nonmatching Pencils

By using nonmatching colored pencils to refine broad sticks, a complex juxtaposed color layer can be quickly created. This can often serve as a final layer; no additional work is needed.

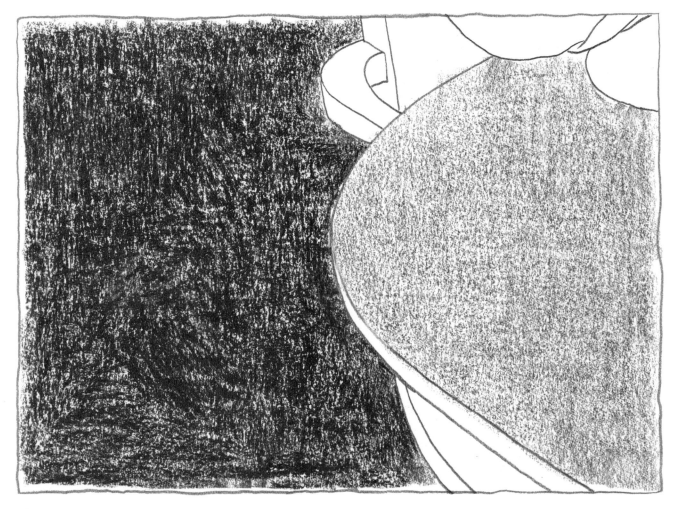

Imagine this to be part of a much larger drawing. As a first step I applied Art Stix in the usual way, but with this difference: Because I wanted to maximize the white flecks of paper in the background, then use a very visible contrasting colored pencil to refine that area, I selected a waxy stick—1902 Ultramarine. This was applied in various directions. For the tabletop, I chose a less waxy 1931 Purple and applied it more carefully for a tighter grain. (See the chart in the Appendix for the relative waxiness of colored pencils and Art Stix.)

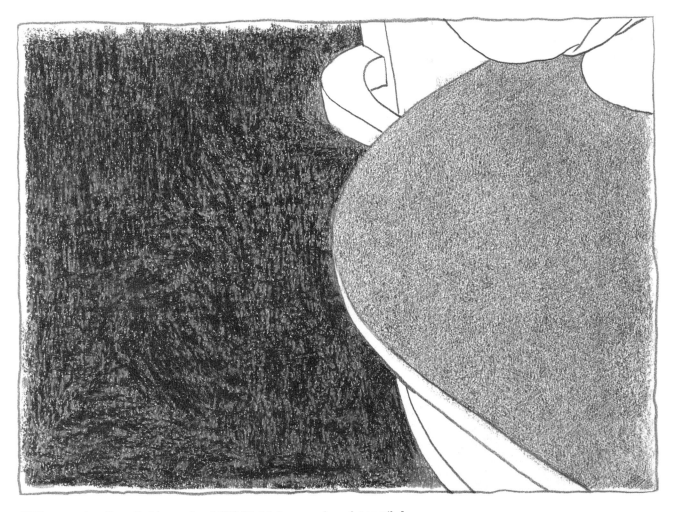

With a contrasting, lighter-valued 992 Light Aqua colored pencil, I quickly added color into the larger white flecks. Surprisingly, this process need not take long to complete, but how far to go with it must remain a matter of personal choice.

The salt-and-pepper mixed-value effect in the background helps to suggest some depth. However, the near-matching value of the 937 Tuscan Red used for refining the purple tabletop helps establish it as a solid plane.

9

SINGLE-LAYER TECHNIQUES

A fast way of handling large areas of color in a drawing is with a single layer of color. The problem with this is that such single layers often tend to be too bright and somewhat simplistic in appearance. Colored pencil layering is in fact generally aimed at avoiding these very pitfalls.

But there are at least three ways of successfully overcoming the disadvantages of single layering and thus saving time. The first is by using the muted effects of low-intensity colors. The second is by juxtaposing colors. And the third is by using an achromatic color such as gray.

As a start toward looking more closely at each of these three options, let's very briefly review what is meant by color intensity.

Color Intensity

Intensity denotes a color's degree of purity, or saturation. It is one of the three dimensions of color, the other two being hue (a color's identity) and value (how light or dark it is).

Low-intensity colors have been diluted—in manufacture or at the time of their use. This dilution can be achieved by combining them with other colors or with neutrals (black, gray or white).

For our purposes, a colored pencil of low intensity can be thought of as containing a color already mixed with another. Using it is like using two or more pencils combined into one.

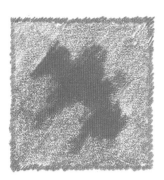 

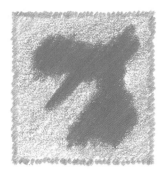 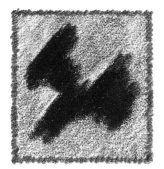

 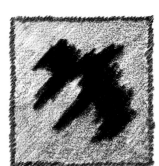

The colors shown at left are of high intensity. Each is relatively pure and saturated. The colors at right are of weaker or lower intensity but are of the same hue families.

Working with Low-Intensity Colors

The colors of large areas are important to any composition. Therefore, it always makes good sense to plan color schemes that take these large areas into account. A quick way of finding low-intensity choices for a color scheme is with the Hue-Value-Intensity Color Charts in the Appendix.

Should you decide to work with an analogous hue scheme of red and red-violet, for example, referring to their charts will show which pencils in these hue families are of low intensity. Narrowing choices in this way makes it easy to select low-intensity colors for single-layer use.

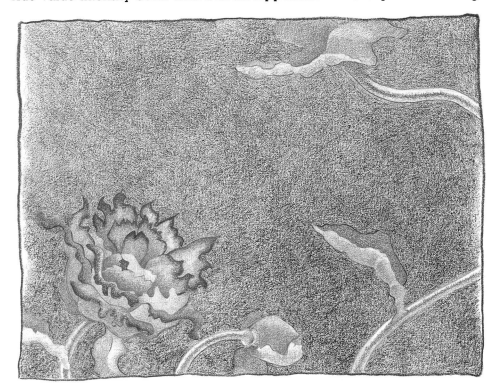

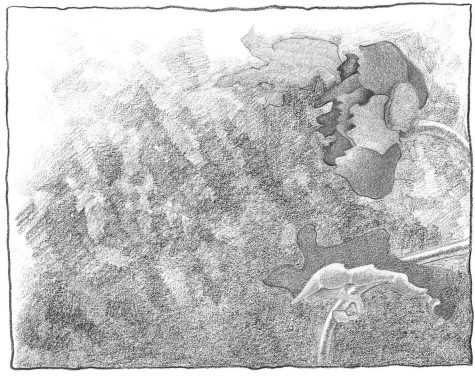

A 948 Sepia pencil—a very low-intensity yellow-orange—applied in a single layer was used in two different ways to indicate negative space. In the top illustration, the layer was applied as an unmodulated middle value. The same pencil was also used in the bottom illustration, but this time the value was modulated.

In most cases, it is a good idea when varying the value of a single color in a large area to avoid values lighter than the lightest value in the subject matter. Another thing to remember is that large and overly dappled negative spaces can easily call too much attention to themselves by appearing too busy.

Working with Juxtaposed Colors

Juxtaposing colors—applying them side by side—was discussed earlier as a time-saving strategy. Single pencil layers of two or more juxtaposed colors are particularly useful for quickly handling large areas.

How each artist selects colors always depends on personal choice and the needs of a color scheme. However, choosing colors for juxtaposition that are closely related in intensity and value can help knit them together. And since a large area is being covered, juxtaposing low-intensity colors results in an additional note of complexity.

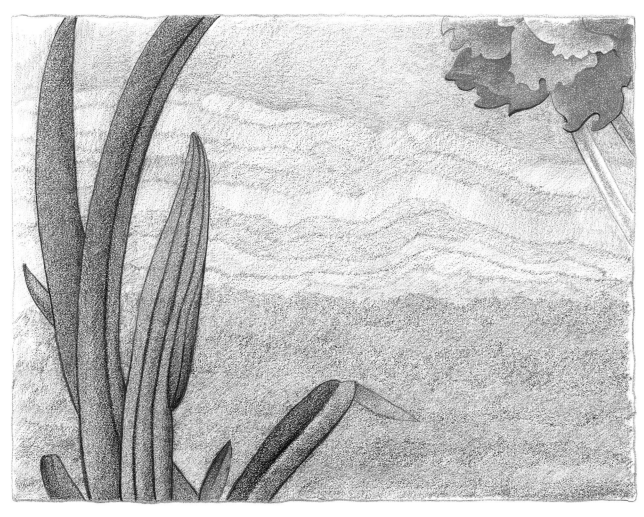

Three low-intensity pencils were used for the large area of negative space in this drawing: 937 Tuscan Red, 945 Sienna Brown, and 947 Burnt Umber. They were not layered but instead were juxtaposed with only scant overlapping.

Working with Grays

Sometimes a large area can be very effectively rendered with an achromatic color such as gray. In fact, grays can be excellent foils for bright colors and often seem to increase the intensity of adjoining tints.

But colored pencils don't mix to gray easily. For this reason, pencil manufacturers offer a variety of grays of different values and temperatures. Prismacolor offers eight such grays (below).

964 WARM GREY VERY LIGHT

968 COLD GREY VERY LIGHT

963 WARM GREY LIGHT

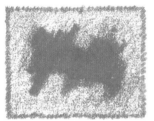

967 COLD GREY LIGHT

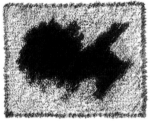

962 WARM GREY MEDIUM

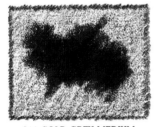

966 COLD GREY MEDIUM

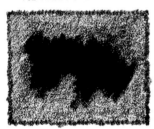

961 WARM GREY DARK

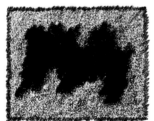

965 COLD GREY DARK

Activating Gray

Gray has a curious power: It may coexist placidly with other colors, or it may take on an elusive color of its own, an approximate complementary of the color nearby. This is called an activated gray. A product of simultaneous contrast, this optical effect occurs when gray is joined with a color of a similar value. Gray remains inactive when joined with a color of a contrasting value.

The above gray is inactive. The same gray below is activated: The adjoining orange color, which is close in value to the gray, causes its bluish complement to appear and disappear in the gray areas. To see this, look first at the orange color, then let your gaze wander within the gray.

10
INJECTING COLOR

"Injecting" color refers to inserting an additional new color into a lightened area. It is similar to the earlier discussed technique of spot-layering but is more appropriate to large, uncomplicated areas and is primarily used to modulate *color* rather than *form*.

Injected color, which has the effect of increasing the richness of an otherwise static passage, can be used in two ways.

1. It can be used after color has been applied to a large area, leaving small intervals as "holes" of much lighter value. Another color is then injected into these lighter areas, creating a subtle (or not so subtle) color change.

2. It can also be employed as a remedy rather than as a preplanned strategy. In this case, a kneaded eraser is used to lighten small portions of an area where a color change or modification is wanted. Additional color is then injected into these newly made intervals of lighter value.

In the example above, a single 931 Purple colored pencil was used for a passage of unmodulated color.

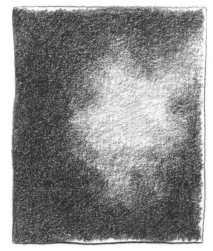

To inject color into a passage, a space must be made for it. This can be done as initial color application proceeds (as shown here) or afterward by lifting pigment away with a kneaded eraser. Note that interior edges are subtly feathered, with no abrupt joining of dark and light values.

A 924 Crimson Red has now been "injected" into the surrounding purple. This modulates the passage's hue and intensity and adds to its overall richness.

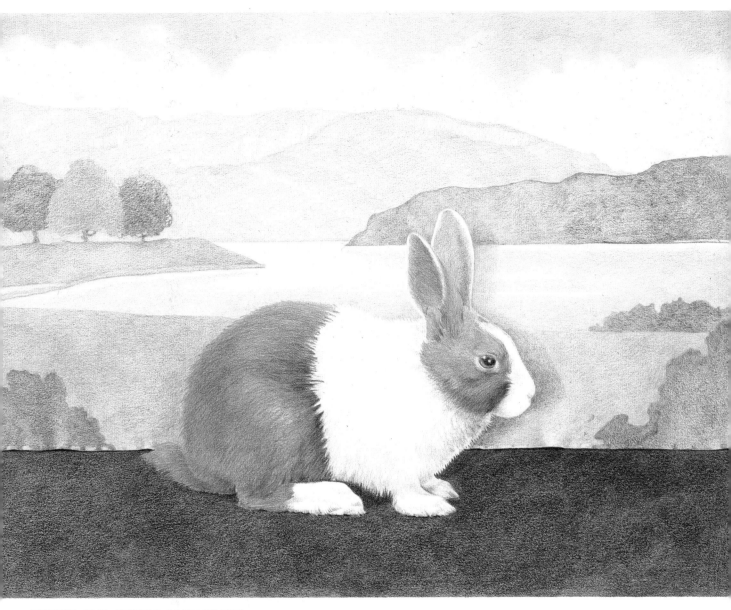

RABBIT AND STUDIO LANDSCAPE
Colored pencil on two-ply Strathmore bristol board, 16″ × 22″ (40.6 cm × 55.9 cm). Collection of Neal and Adrienne Salomon, Portland, Oregon.

In this drawing, injected color was used to enrich the blue-violet of the floor. Two colors—933 Blue Violet and 931 Purple—were used to establish the plane of the floor. Several small areas in this plane were left lighter in anticipation of injecting a third color. A 923 Scarlet Lake was then feathered into the light areas. Values were kept the same so the solidity of the floor itself would not be compromised.

Step-By-Step
INJECTING COLOR

My goal will be to make simple layers of color within the large areas of this drawing appear to contain a richness usually achieved by more complex layering.

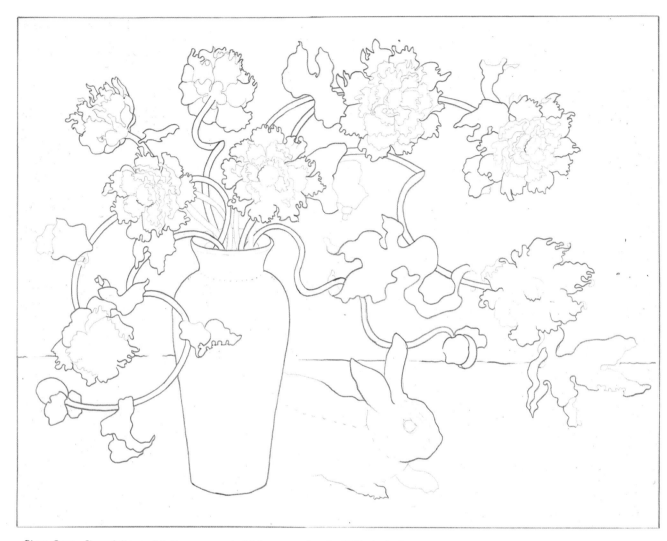

Step One. *Graphite guidelines were laid in on a sheet of Westwinds paper. The image size is 18¾" × 24½", a relatively large size for a drawing, and ordinarily I would simply use Art Stix to save time. But in this case the background is very fragmented, due to the floral design, and I cannot depend on Art Stix alone. I will save time instead by using a simple two-layer approach, with a third color injected in just a few areas for more interesting hue variations.*

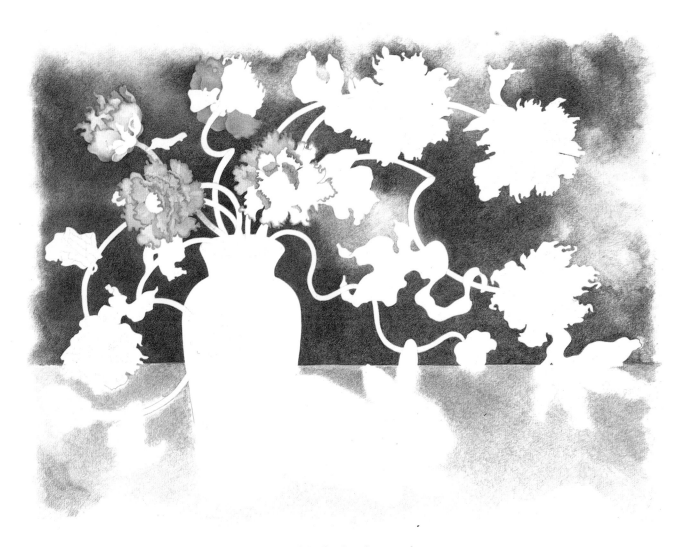

Step Two. Some color has now been developed in the background, on the tabletop, and in a few of the flowers. Specifically, here's what is happening in the background:

A 901 Indigo Blue was applied, leaving some areas much lighter in value than others. These areas can be clearly seen in the upper right side of the drawing. In the left side, I've begun applying a second layer, this time of 937 Tuscan Red. It has been applied with varying pressure over the blue, except in the open "holes." I have "injected" a 931 Purple into these light areas. Because the small areas were very light, the purple asserts itself very clearly.

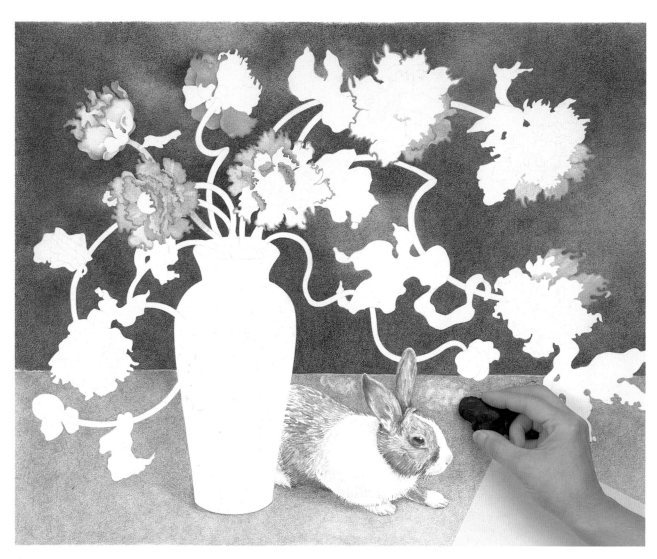

Step Three. The second layer of 937 Tuscan Red was applied to the rest of the background, and the remaining light areas were injected with 931 Purple. The result is a gradual modulation of hue, value, and intensity.

The rabbit was also begun, using linear strokes of various reds and oranges, and the tabletop's second color, 901 Indigo Blue, has been applied over the first layer of 941 Raw Umber. Some of the color is being lifted away from this area with a kneaded eraser, in preparation for the injection of what I now believe is a needed cooler note toward the back.

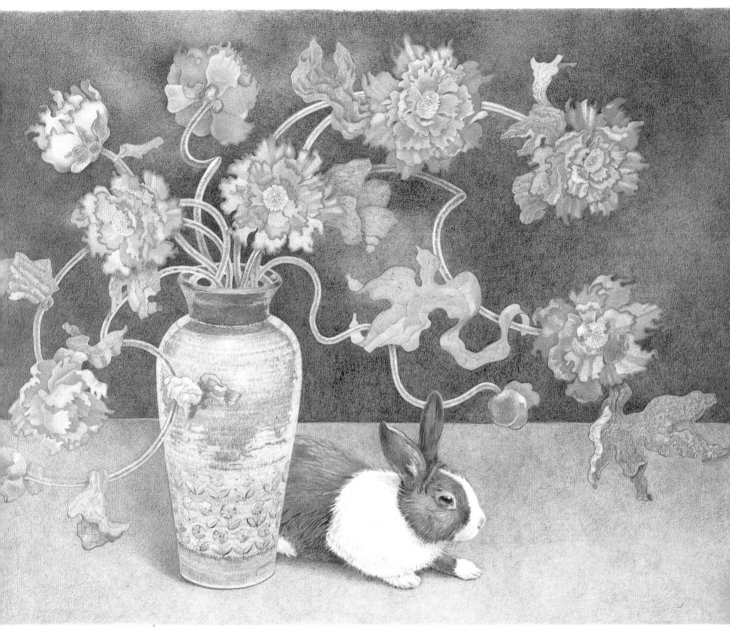

RABBIT AND FLOWERS
Colored pencil on Westwinds paper, 18¾″ × 24½″ (47.6 cm × 62.2 cm). Private collection.

Step Four. To finish this drawing, the vase and flowers were completed. The rabbit was softened with more color applied tonally over its linear stage.

When I assessed the background, the injected purple seemed about right; no adjustment was needed. How much an injected color shows will always depend on how light the "hole" for it was allowed to remain and on the color chosen for this purpose. To cool the rear area of the tabletop, constructed with 941 Raw Umber under 901 Indigo Blue, some of the raw umber had to be removed. This was done by lifting away both colors and injecting 901 Indigo Blue. Because indigo blue was the original second layer, it blends in very subtly.

11

AN IMPRIMATURA TECHNIQUE

Imprimatura is an Italian word that refers to the staining of a surface preparatory to painting on it. For our purposes, we may think of imprimatura as a tonal application of color to all or most of a surface before a drawing is begun on it.

This preparatory layer, applied rapidly with a colored pencil or broad stick of color, can become the first layer of color for a drawing's subject and can also serve as its background, often with little or no further work.

An added dividend of imprimatura—besides a drastic reduction in background layering time—is that a single color, common to all further mixtures, usually helps unite any drawing's overall hue scheme.

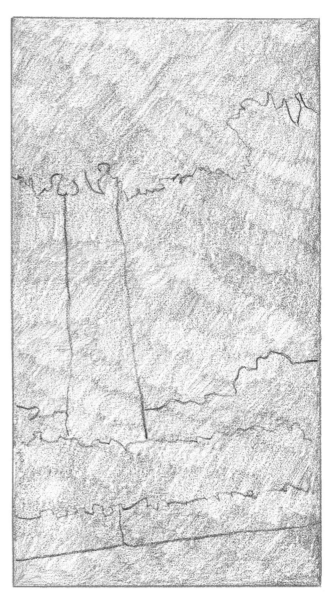

Here is an imprimatura applied prior to drawing. It can be given a textural look (as shown) or not, as a matter of personal choice. This imprimatura and those for the two following drawings were made with a 903 True Blue pencil, using medium pressure.

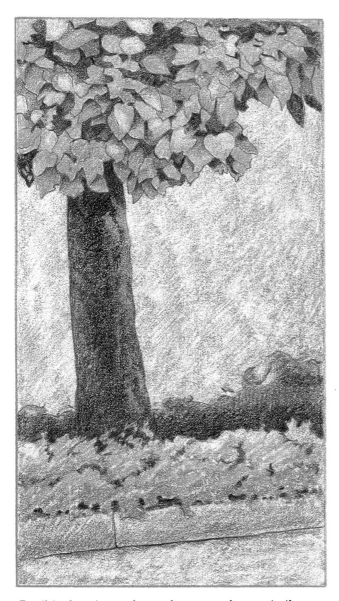

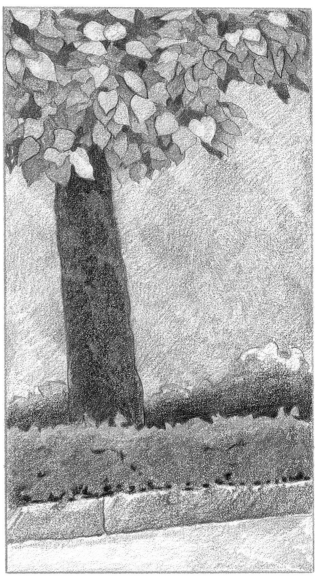

For this drawing, a hue scheme analogous to the imprimatura was chosen. The leaves and shrubs were drawn with various greens, and some of the imprimatura was allowed to show. No changes or refinements have been added to the original 903 True Blue of the background.

In this drawing—still with the same kind of imprimatura—a warm color scheme contrasts with the background. A kneaded eraser was used to lighten various areas of the imprimatura. Then a 932 Violet pencil was spot-layered into some of the lightened areas to enrich the background.

Step-By-Step
IMPRIMATURA TECHNIQUE

A drawing to be built on an imprimatura begins much like any other, with perhaps only a partial idea and a few thumbnail sketches. But it differs from other drawings in one very important way: It is critical that a color scheme be worked out ahead of time to ensure that the chosen imprimatura can successfully serve as a first layer for both background and subject.

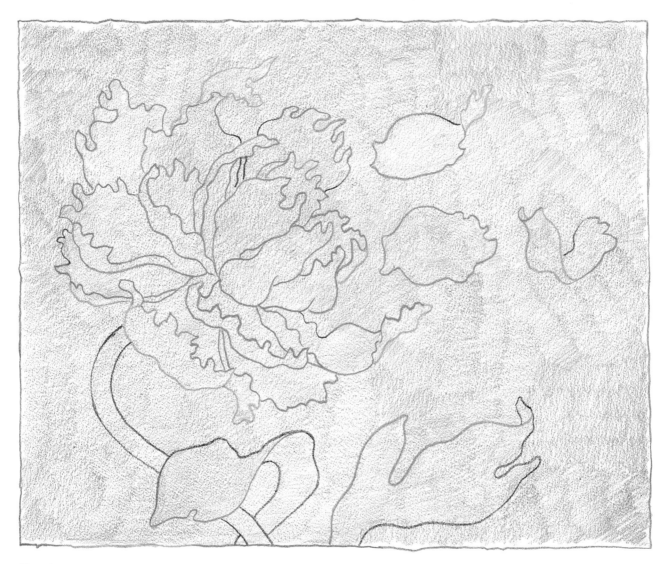

Step One. *An analogous color scheme of red and red-violet was planned for this small drawing. I applied a layer of 931 Purple to the entire surface of a sheet of Strathmore bristol board. This imprimatura layer was done quickly and the strokes go in all directions; I made no attempt to refine gestural texture. Over this, I drew the simple outlines of my drawing's image with colored pencil.*

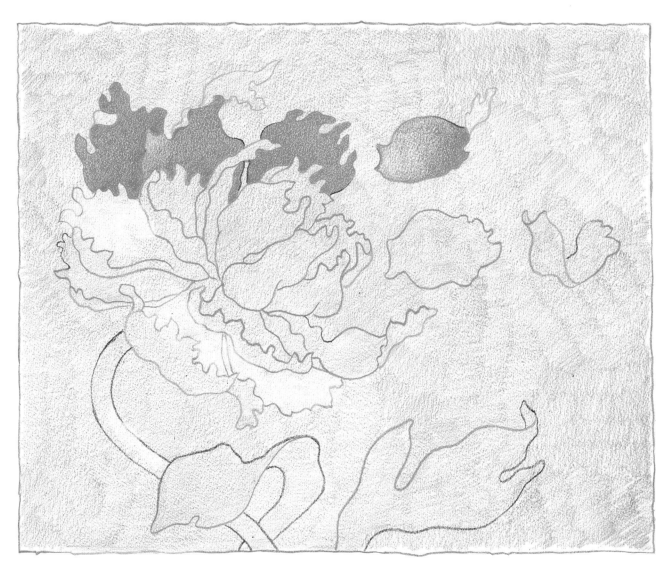

Step Two. *A 923 Scarlet Lake was applied to the flower petals and a 931 Purple spot-layered into it for some alayeral effects. With a kneaded eraser, I also lifted away a portion of the imprimatura in the foreground petals so that when I applied the same 923 Scarlet Lake to them they would appear brighter than the petals above.*

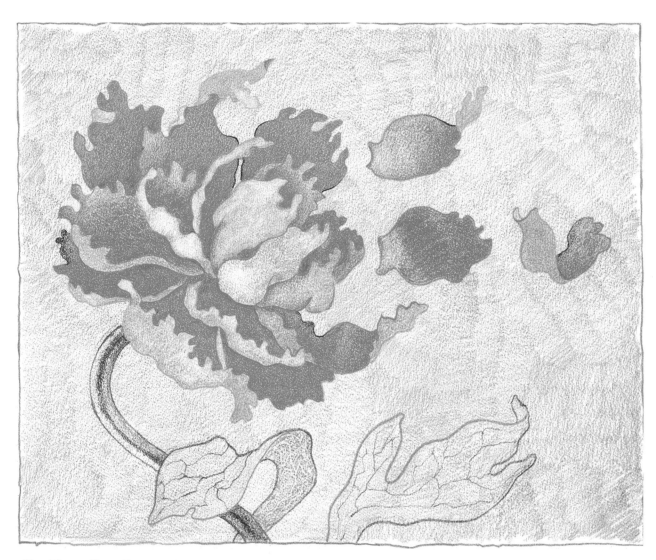

Step Three. *The other petals have now been brought to the same point as the first ones, using the same techniques and colors—923 Scarlet Lake for the petals and 931 Purple for dark values. A 918 Orange was also applied to the petals' undersides, and a 912 Apple Green and 911 Olive Green were used linearly to establish the veins and undersides of the leaves. All these colors mix well with the original imprimatura layer, causing their separate intensities to be somewhat muted.*

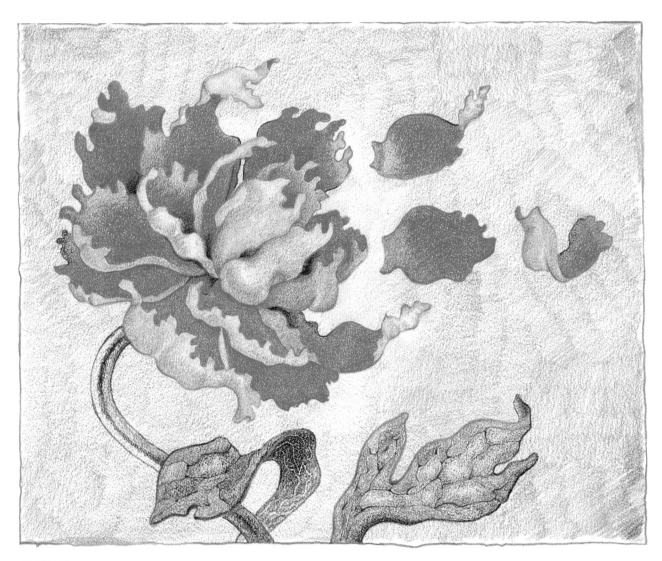

PEONY
Colored pencil on paper, 6⅛" × 5⅝" (15.6 cm × 13.2 cm). Collection of Mr. and Mrs. Thomas Caddy, Troutdale, Oregon.

Step Four. *After assessing the values in this drawing, I decided to lift away and lighten some of the imprimatura in the center. Using the 901 Indigo Blue, I also darkened some of the flower's petals. This helped stretch the value range.*

A sharp 922 Scarlet Red pencil was used to further reduce the white grain of the paper, making the flower colors appear more saturated. Some of the petal forms were developed further, and the leaves were modeled with a single tonal layer of several related juxtaposed colors.

The only modifications of the original imprimatura in this drawing are a lightening in the foreground petals, a small value change at the center, and a final slight darkening at the drawing's right corners for balance.

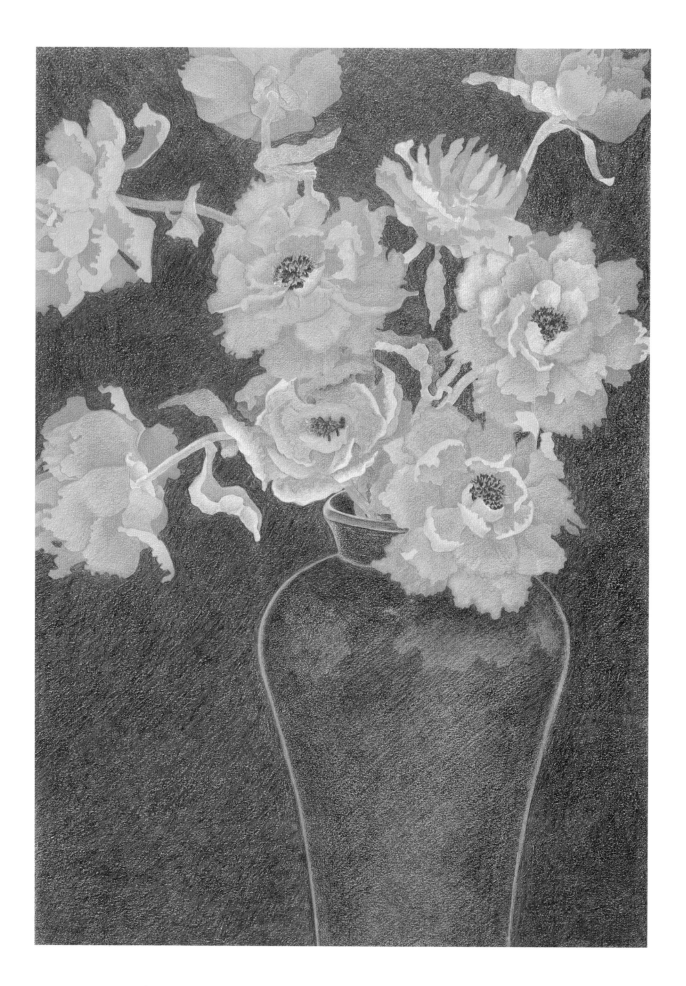

12

GAINING COMPLEXITY WITH A TEXTURAL CHANGE

A unique characteristic of colored pencils is that their appearance seems to change depending on the reflectivity of the drawing surface. This means that if we alter or "distress" parts of a surface before drawing on it, we can add more complexity of texture and color to even a single color layer.

We can do this very simply and quickly, after the main elements of a drawing are indicated, by using a white or light-colored pencil to make a series of marks or patterns throughout a large area. Color work is then begun as usual, ignoring the barely visible marks. But each time the pencil crosses a waxy mark, the pencil's color and textural look are slightly altered. The net result is a single layer of color that looks as if it were constructed of multiple layers.

This describes the process in its simplest terms. With some experimentation on your own, you may discover a number of subtle and swiftly made textural and color changes of this kind.

A  B

In A (above), a 938 White was used to distress the surface before a 992 Light Aqua was applied. In B, the distressing pencil was a 914 Cream. Pencil pressure for both the white and the cream was medium at the top and firm at the bottom. With this technique, paper hardness will affect the result. Both these examples were drawn on medium-soft Westwinds paper.

NIGHT BOUQUET II
Colored pencil on three-ply Strathmore
bristol board, 18½" × 13"
(47.0 cm × 13.0 cm). Collection of L'Ermitage
Hotel, Beverly Hills, California.

At an early stage in this drawing, the negative space was distressed with a white pencil. Two layers of color were then applied, revealing a texture that appears lost and found depending on how it is viewed.

Step-By-Step
A SURFACE-DISTRESSING TECHNIQUE

This illustration is designed to suggest a detail within a larger drawing. The background will consist of a single layer of color, but the paper itself will be altered to make the color appear varied.

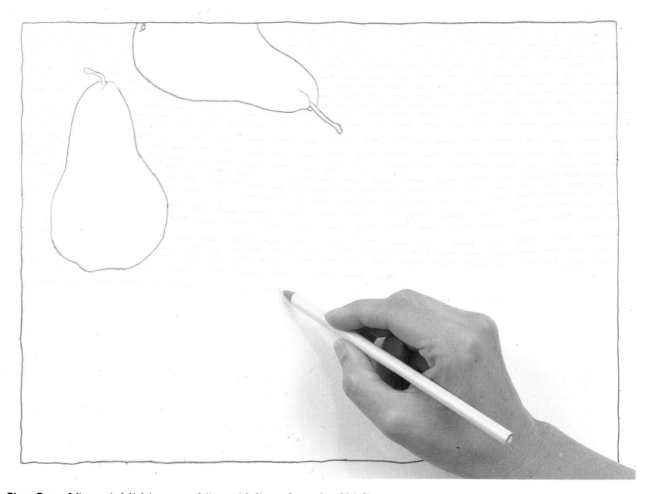

Step One. *After establishing graphite guidelines, I used a 914 Cream pencil to quickly apply a broken stripe pattern in the negative space only. This mark is somewhat structured, and I didn't want it to become too assertive, so I applied the cream pencil lightly, just enough to make slick dashes of wax.*

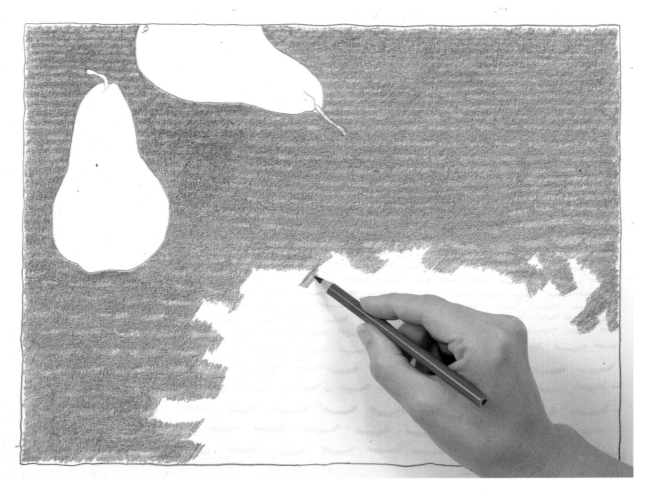

Step Two. With a 931 Purple pencil I applied a fairly dense single layer of color, disregarding the waxy marks. Regardless of how lightly or heavily this layer is applied, its color will be affected each time it crosses over the waxy mark of the cream pencil.

In the close-up view, the cream-colored marks can be clearly seen through the overall purple layer. Had the marks been made with a white pencil, the purple would have taken on a cooler cast.

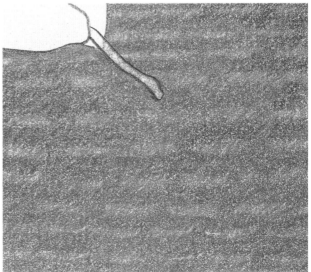

13

WHEN AND HOW A WHITE BACKGROUND WORKS

Leaving background areas blank can save you a great deal of time. But in color drawing, the key to making a white background work is to actively plan for it, rather than let it occur by default. When a white background is to be used, it is critical that the color scheme and composition be designed for it. To sidestep such planning is to practically guarantee poor results.

Difficulties with White Backgrounds

There are at least two major reasons why white backgrounds can be disappointing:

1. Almost nothing in nature is flat white. Therefore, an expanse of white in an otherwise hue-laden drawing looks false and contrasts too much with the colors and modeled forms. An unyielding white opacity is often simply too raw—even snow and the lightest of highlights contain many delicate and modulated tints.

2. White dominates in a design. Because white is expansive and thus appears to come forward, a large white background can confuse and diminish a drawing's subject. Areas of brilliant white can also darken nearby colors and weaken their luminosity.

How to Make White Backgrounds Work

To successfully use white backgrounds with color drawings, it is necessary to focus carefully on your composition and color scheme.

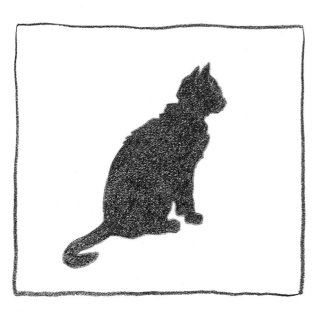 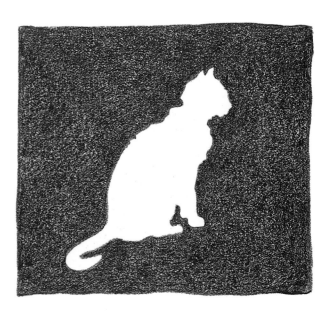

There are inherent problems with using flat white effectively as a background. These occur because white is one of the two extremes in the value scale and is profoundly expansive. This can be clearly seen in the two small drawings above.

The black cat at left contracts and looks like a small cutout within the white field. The white also seems to come forward around the cat. In the example at right, the whiteness of the cat brings it forward, and it appears larger than the black cat although it is really slightly smaller.

It is unusual for an artist to remove a subject from at least a suggestion of its usual context. When this is done—as it is so handsomely by botanical and scientific illustrators—we instantly know that we are being shown a specimen that has been deliberately removed from its environment and presented for greater clarity against a blank or nonessential background.

Two factors will help you successfully integrate a colored subject and a white backdrop:

1. Minimize white negative space. The size of a white background can have a profound effect on its power.

2. Minimize contrasts between colored positive and white negative space. It is often possible to arrange fragments or shapes of white within a subject. Soft edges or sketchy outside contour lines can also help ease transitions between subject and background.

Color schemes are also important when you are using a white background. White is a powerful ele-ment, and it is worth the time it takes to plan a color scheme for it. If you decide, for instance, to work with a split-complementary color scheme and no background, you must think of white as an active member of the color team.

It is also worth noting that some art theorists believe there to be an affinity between white and the upper end of the hue spectrum, blue-green through violet. This theory, if correct, implies that a bluish color may harmonize well with white, while a color near the other end of the spectrum, such as brown, may create tension. The important thing here, of course, is not which effect is better (either can be) but being able to plan it.

Still another consideration is that paper itself has temperature. White drawing papers can range from bluish (with names like polar or arctic white) to yellowish (such as warm or antique white). Some artists prefer a cool white because with time and exposure to light such a paper will probably grow warmer. A paper that has a warm cast to begin with, on the other hand, may eventually become too yellow.

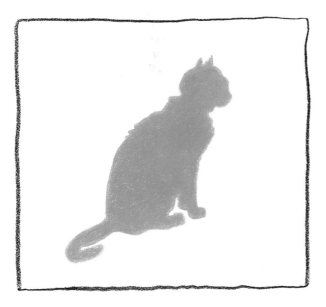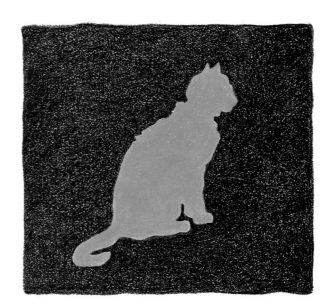

Our perception of color is dynamic; it depends a great deal on what adjoins or surrounds it. Large areas of white often have a predictable influence on nearby colors.

The two drawings above illustrate how white tends to darken color and reduce luminosity. Both cats were drawn with 913 Green Bice at full pressure, and they are physically identical. But in the drawing at left, the color of the cat appears darker due to the brilliance of the white background. And the luminosity of the green—so visible in the drawing at right—has been extinguished.

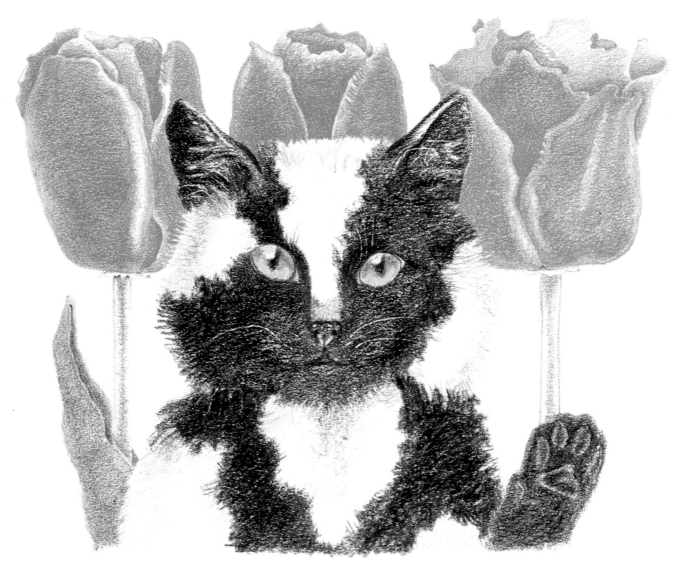

CAT OF PROSPERITY
Colored pencil on two-ply Strathmore bristol board, 5½" × 7" (14.0 cm × 17.8 cm). Private collection.

This drawing relies on two strategies for dealing with the white background. One is an arrangement of elements—a composition—designed to minimize the amount of white negative space. The other is based on the fact that a white background often works well with a color drawing that has strong black and white elements. A possible explanation for this is that we are accustomed to seeing drawings in black and white media (graphite, ink, charcoal) with little or no background.

Technically, the black parts of the cat are layered blue and brown, the red-orange blooms are a major element, and green foliage is also included. But the dominant feeling of the color scheme is black and white—which we easily accept with only white paper as negative space.

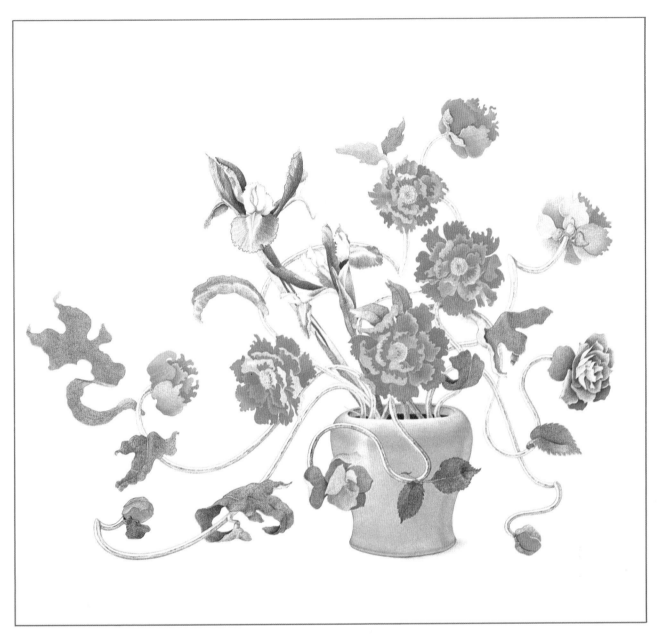

WHITE FLORAL #3
Colored pencil on Rising museum board, 31″ × 38″ (78.7 cm × 96.5 cm). Collection of
L'Ermitage Hotel, Beverly Hills, California.

This drawing—one of a series of florals on white backgrounds—relies
heavily on a compositional strategy to help soften the transitions between positive and negative space. The strategy was to arrange white
shapes within a subject. While the white is not actually a part of the
floral forms, the meandering stems corral and embrace enough negative space to make it seem part of the subject's color.

The color scheme was also planned with a white background in
mind. Because the cool end of the spectrum appears to be compatible
with white, the color scheme has been kept cool; even the scarlet
flowers have been cooled with some lavender petals.

14

USING A VIGNETTE

The vignette is characterized by a gradual reduction or fading away of some of a drawing's peripheral elements; it is essentially a means of transition between subject and background. This device can save time because it lessens work on the background. Artists use it to emphasize a center of interest, and it is a familiar device in portraiture, where the background must not be allowed to distract from the face. It can also impart an air of informality and spontaneity.

While there are many techniques for producing an effective vignette, one tenet seems constant: A truly successful vignette cannot be merely imposed on or done to a drawing. It must instead flow out of or seem to emanate from the subject itself. A good vignette has a look of having suddenly—almost accidentally—happened. Actually, the traditional drawing strokes for producing it are more likely to have been carefully developed and practiced, and they are a major factor in the overall mood of the drawing.

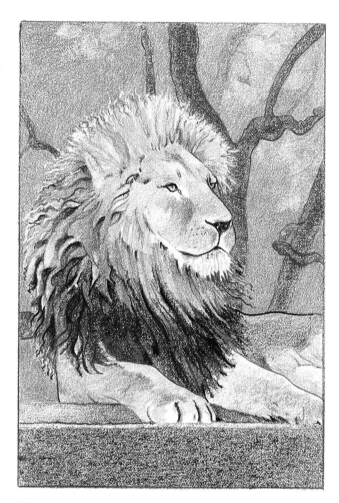

These small color drawings show a subject with three kinds of background, two of them vignettes. Both the foreground and the background of the first drawing are fully rendered. It contains the kind of simple and straightforward subject, however, that seems likely to lend itself to a vignette technique.

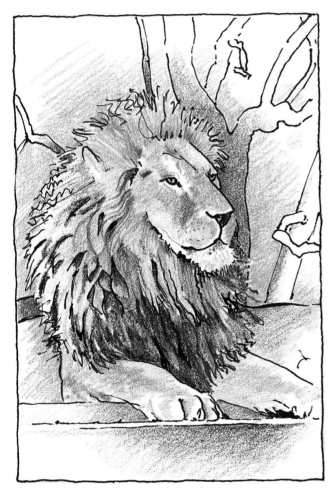

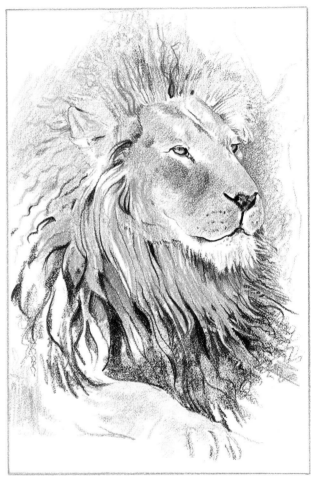

This time the subject was composed as in the first version, but ink was used to establish much of the drawing in a linear fashion. Color was then applied tonally within the lion—the drawing's center of interest—and some of it spills out into the other elements. It helps, when incorporating a great deal of white in background and foreground, to also allow some white to remain in the subject for a smoother integration of elements.

For this second vignette, the lion's head was composed somewhat larger within the total frame of reference. The background and foreground were deemphasized further and retain only a suggestion of their original colors. Again, white was allowed to remain in some of the subject—notably the lion's mane—to soften the contrast between positive and negative space. This type of vignette is frequently used in portraiture.

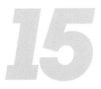

COLORED SURFACES

Colored pencil work on a colored surface often has a quiet and richly luminous look. Working on a colored surface can also increase drawing speed. The three main factors that contribute to this are: a colored surface can itself serve as a drawing's negative space; layering time is sharply reduced when a colored surface becomes the first layer of color; and the value of a colored surface functions as part of a drawing's total value range.

The most familiar colored surface for drawing is colored paper. One widely available brand is Canson Mi Teintes, which offers 35 colors of varying values and intensities and is considered very light resistant.

A second type of colored drawing surface is colored mat board. Drawing on these boards—which were originally designed for matting artwork—is a somewhat new development. Many of them now meet conservation standards, and their drawing surfaces have excellent resilience for layering, as well as for a variety of more exotic techniques.

Hand-colored boards are yet another type of colored surface. These are usually the product of personal experimentation. One method for preparing a hand-colored surface is brushing tube acrylic thinned with water onto a high-quality illustration board. Plain water is then brushed onto its back, and the painted board is clipped against another flat, sturdy board to dry. An advantage of hand-colored boards is that their color can be much less flat in appearance than that of most ready-made supports.

Selecting Colored Papers

Colored drawing papers are too often selected on the basis of hue alone, even though intensity and value can actually be far more important.

Paper colors that are too intense can overwhelm any colored pencil work done on them. A paper's value can also present serious problems. Fortunately, the effect a colored paper's value is likely to have on a colored pencil drawing is fairly predictable. Here are a few guidelines:

Light value range. Colored papers in this group tend to darken pencil colors. A drawing with many light passages would probably suffer. Low-key work is better suited to these values.

Middle value range. There is a long tradition of using colored or neutral papers in this group. A full value range can quickly be expressed with one light and one dark pencil.

Dark value range. It is with these values of colored papers that colored pencils can appear their most luminous.

Black paper. This represents an extreme in the value range, and even though black papers are not truly black, working on them can mean contending with a great deal of unmodulated dark value. Also, while it would seem that the paper's own dark value could be a drawing's darkest value, this is not always so. Because even the darkest papers are not actually all that dark, a 901 Indigo Blue or a 935 Black is still needed for a truly dark note.

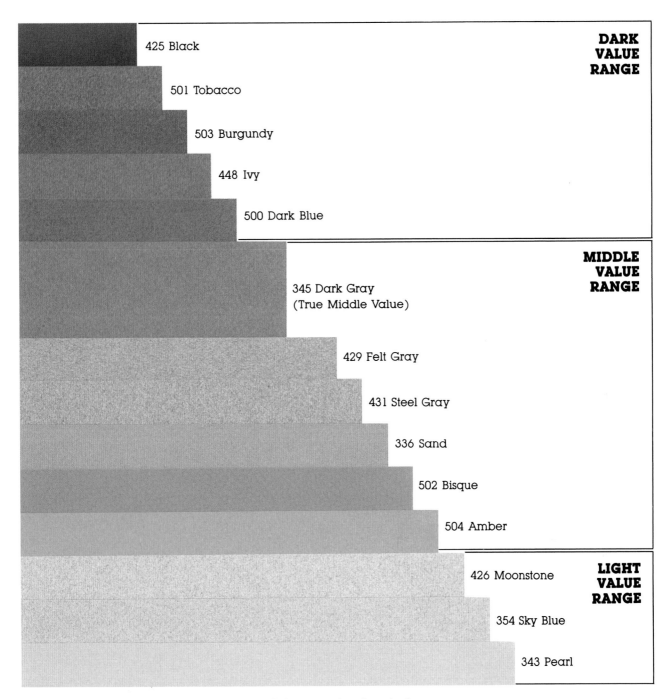

425 Black

501 Tobacco

503 Burgundy

448 Ivy

500 Dark Blue

345 Dark Gray
(True Middle Value)

429 Felt Gray

431 Steel Gray

336 Sand

502 Bisque

504 Amber

426 Moonstone

354 Sky Blue

343 Pearl

Colored Papers. There are many kinds and degrees of surface texture among the various brands of colored papers. Some papers also have less texture on one side than on the other. Colored pencils generally perform best on colored papers with very little texture.

These fourteen samples of colored paper are from the Canson Mi Teintes line and are particularly useful with colored pencils. It is interesting to note that although the colors shown have been divided into their relative value groups, all are actually within or very close to a middle range on a true value chart.

Selecting a Palette

Pencil colors can appear dramatically unlike their customary selves on various colored papers. For this reason, each colored paper may require a different colored pencil palette.

A good way to cope with this complication is to simply experiment with pencil colors on actual swatches of the colored paper to be used. Shown here, for example, are a group of identical pencils applied to a white and three colored papers.

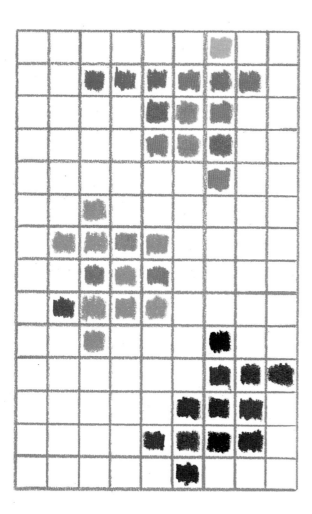

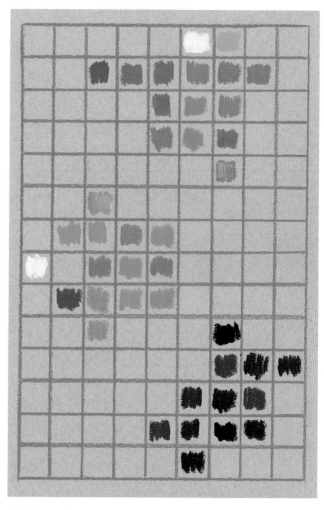

White Paper. *This first grid shows how we are accustomed to seeing our pencil colors. There are three approximate groupings within it: one of six dark colored pencils, a second of six cool pencils, and another of eight warm pencils.*

343 Pearl (Light Value Range). *Some of the pencil colors here begin to appear more vivid than those on the white paper, but not as much so as on the two darker papers. The pink grid itself appears darker here than on the darker papers but lighter than on the white. It is now necessary to add white (or a very light color) to get a light color.*

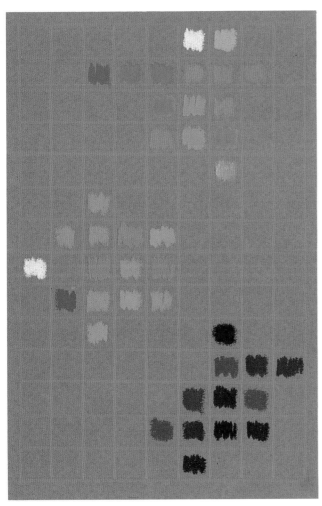

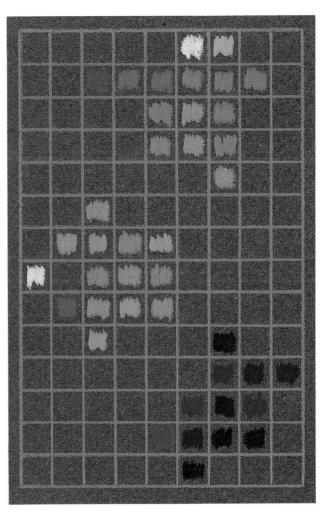

502 Bisque (Middle Value Range). *With this paper, another complication is suddenly present. The paper itself has a very definite hue—ochre—which mixes with the pencil colors. The warm red-orange pencils are analogous with the paper; their colors are intensified. The cool blue-green group, however, is nearly complementary; pencil colors in this group seem to vibrate. The pink grid—because it is so similar in hue and value to the paper—takes on some of that mysterious quality a closely related color often attains as it becomes nearly invisible.*

501 Tobacco (Dark Value Range). *It is on darker papers such as this that pencil colors become most luminous. Compare this pink grid with the three other pink grids. Also present is a kind of clarity that occurs when pencil colors are vivid and contrast well with a surface. Although such contrast can be very high with white paper, a white paper's own brilliance often reduces the vividness of the pencils. This does not happen when the same pencils are used on a dark surface.*

16
ENLISTING OTHER MEDIA

A great attraction of the colored pencil medium for many artists is its simplicity and lack of paraphernalia. But there are also ways of saving time by adding a bit of equipment and technique from other media.

Aqueous colors, for example, can be used to quickly lay in backgrounds or large areas. This can be done with a brush and liquid acrylic or watercolor. (It can also be done with an airbrush, but the expense of equipment and specialized training put this method outside the scope of this discussion.)

There are two basic problems when aqueous media are used with colored pencils. The first—which is obvious and fairly easily managed—is that highlight passages must be reserved. Once an area is covered, there is no easy way to regain paper highlights.

The second and much trickier problem is that the granular appearance of colored pencil is dramatically different from that of painted color. Without adequate transition or blending, this can present a serious gap in a drawing's unity and credibility. In this chapter, we will examine this major problem and some of our options for dealing with it.

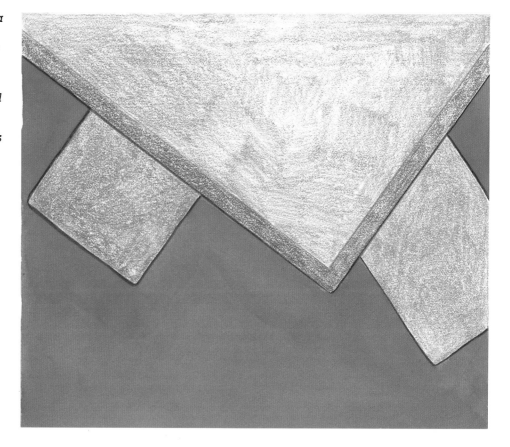

The Problem. *Two media have been used here—with very different looks. The red area is liquid acrylic color, applied with a red sable brush. Colored pencil was used for the angular blue, green, and pink shapes. The acrylic portion looks thoroughly saturated, with no white paper flecks. The colored pencil areas do not. If two such distinctly different looking areas are to work together successfully in a single drawing, they must be blended better.*

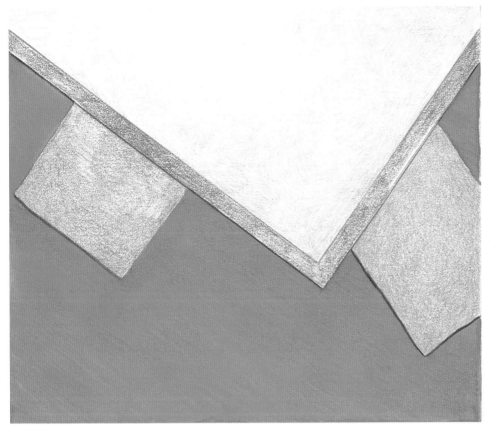

Option One. *In both these examples, the liquid acrylic and colored pencil were applied as before, but then a layer of colored pencil was applied over the red acrylic. In the top drawing, the pencil color is similar to the color of the acrylic. In the lower example, a completely different pencil color was loosely applied. In both cases the uncompromising quality of the acrylic has been softened, and a granular quality similar to that of colored pencil has been added. This helps unify the two media. (Notice that while the grain of colored pencil is usually white, colored pencils over acrylic produce a colored grain.)*

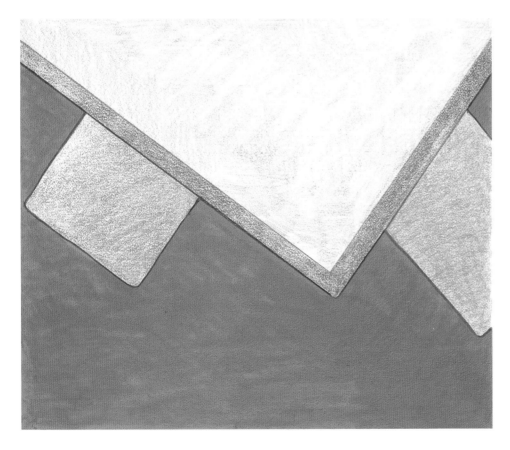

Option Two. This time, liquid acrylic color was used first to establish the entire drawing, then colored pencil was applied over it to refine the image. Overall unity with this method is very good. The principles for selecting pencil colors to layer over painted colors are similar to those used with colored papers.

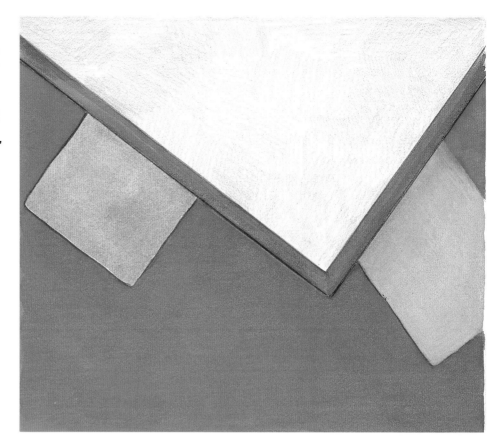

Option Three. In this example, the red liquid acrylic was not covered with colored pencil. Instead, the angular colored pencil shapes were applied with very heavy pencil pressure, flattening the paper so that no granular white flecks show. The elements look well integrated and their colors are nicely intense. A drawback of this method is that applying constant heavy pencil pressure is arduous work and invites wax buildup.

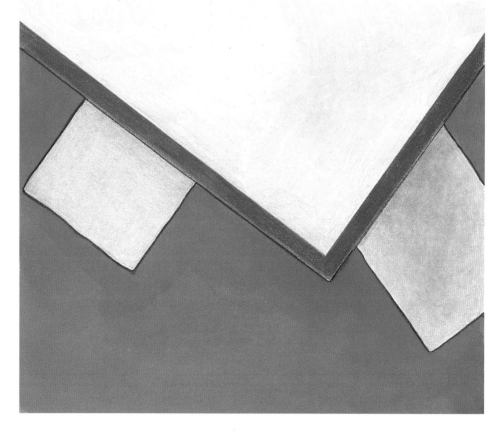

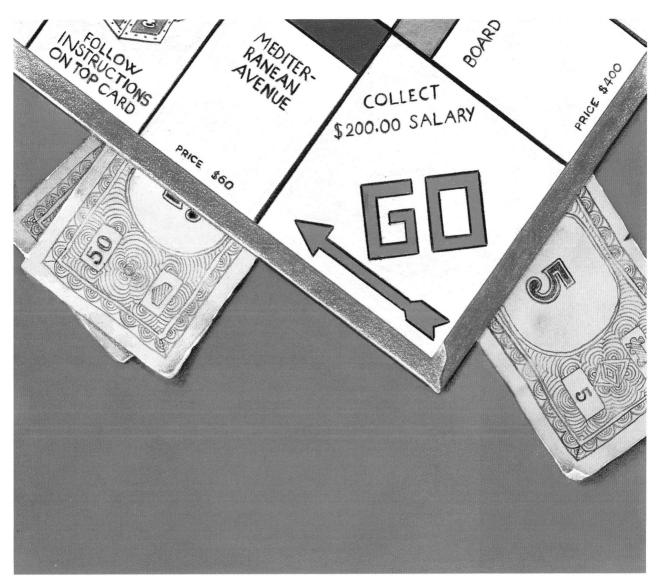

Option Four. A combination of the other options was used for this more developed illustration. Red, light blue, and pink liquid acrylic colors were first used to establish the background and the play money. That was the total extent of the aqueous medium. Colored pencils were then used to render the remaining elements. Some of the pencil was applied with heavy pressure to relate it to the liquid color; some was used lightly for more granularity. As a final step, colored pencil was used tonally over the red acrylic and linearly over the blue and pink to render details of the money. This is a fast technique, and the dual nature of the separate media is now effectively masked.

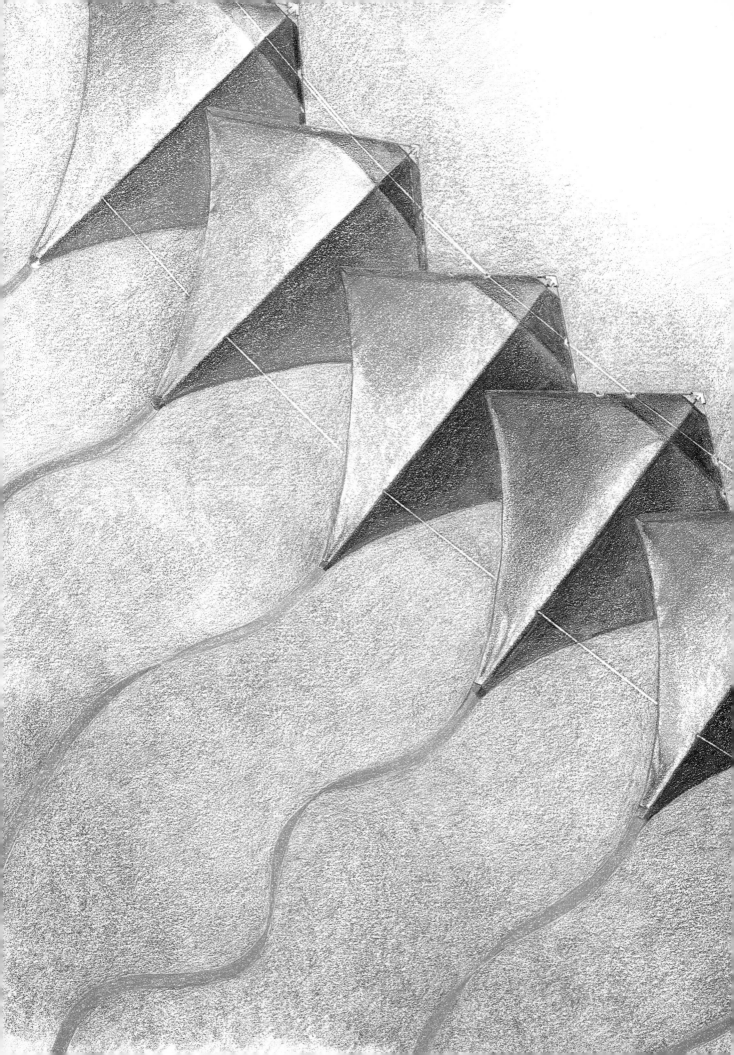

REFINING YOUR OWN WORKING METHODS

The purpose of Part Three is to offer aid in finding one's own opportunities for gaining speed when desired. After reviewing some good practices used in drawing, and also in and around the studio, we will discuss a simple but practical means for trouble-shooting your own working methods.

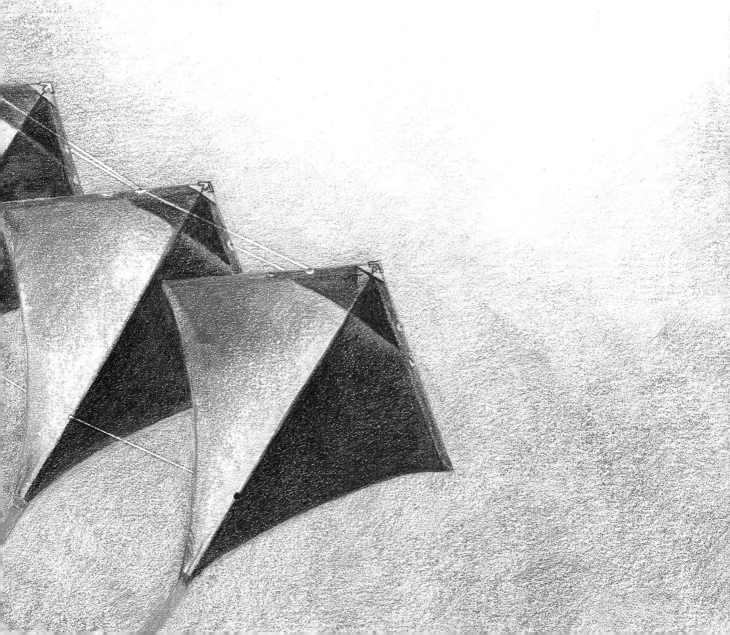

17
DRAWING TIPS

Besides the major time-saving techniques outlined in the previous chapters, you can often find smaller ways to draw more efficiently with colored pencils. A few of the tips that follow offer immediate time savings. Other suggestions do not but are directed instead at avoiding the later delays of correcting a mistake or stopping in frustration. Some of these strategies may also serve as a beginning toward finding ways you can smooth out your own personal working methods.

Signing in a Dark Surround
Colored pencil drawings are usually signed within the picture itself, rather than in the margin. Because it can be difficult to do this in a dark area, signatures are sometimes "forced" into awkward places. One less-than-satisfactory solution to signing in an appropriate but dark area is lightening the area with a kneaded eraser—which can ruin the area's continuity. A better way is to use an impressed line technique for the signature.

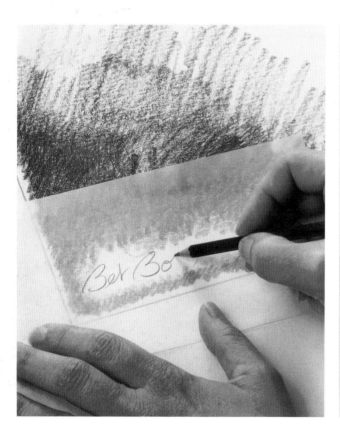

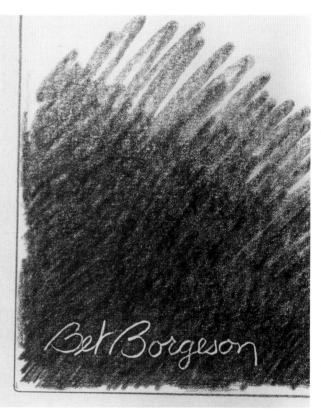

Impressing a Signature. A signature can be easily impressed into the appropriate area before the dark color is added. Cover the drawing with tracing paper and sign your name, using a graphite pencil and pressing down firmly. Remove the tracing paper and complete the dark passage. The signature will remain white and be clearly visible against the dark background.

In this example, the signature is white. For a colored line, a light layer of color could have been applied to the signature area before beginning the impressing step.

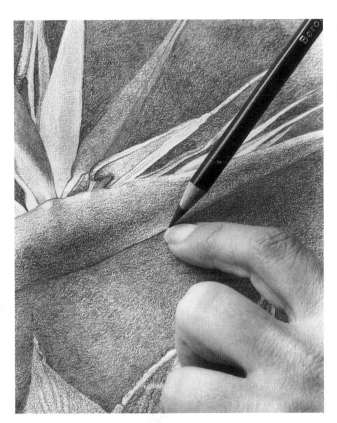

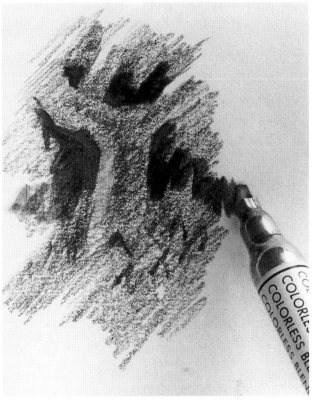

Working to an Edge. *Many artists use a ruler as a barrier for stopping multiple pencil strokes along a straight edge, but a fingernail can also serve this purpose. With a bit of practice, you can learn to easily and rapidly move your finger in unison with the pencil along a curving edge.*

Quick Darks. *A colorless blender (no. 311 Design Marker) can instantly darken small areas of colored pencil without creating wax buildup. This marker, which has no color of its own, contains a solvent that liquefies the colored pencil binder, making areas of pencil work flow together and darken. It dries to a matte finish, however, and a few pencil strokes are needed afterward to restore the sheen. (Remember to use any solvent only in a well-ventilated area and for no more than a few minutes at a time.)*

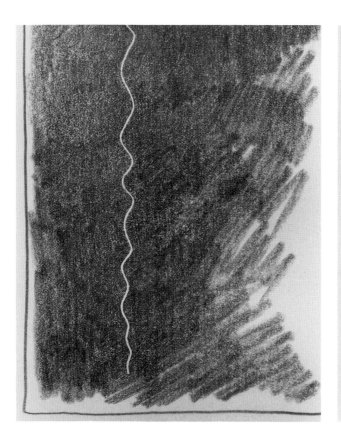

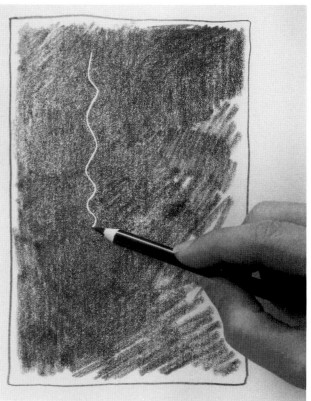

Erasing an Impressed Line. *Sometimes you may want to remove impressed lines that seem overdone or in the wrong places or that were impressed accidentally. Despite the fact that an impressed line tends to produce a very pronounced mark, its effect can be "erased" or greatly muted.*

In this case the impressed line has been approximately half removed, beginning from the bottom. The "erasing" was done by sharpening the same colored pencil used for the surrounding area and running it lightly along inside the groove. The telltale reminder of a filled-in line is not the groove itself but the tiny ridges of piled-up color on each side of it. These can be concealed by slightly darkening the areas alongside the line to match the ridges.

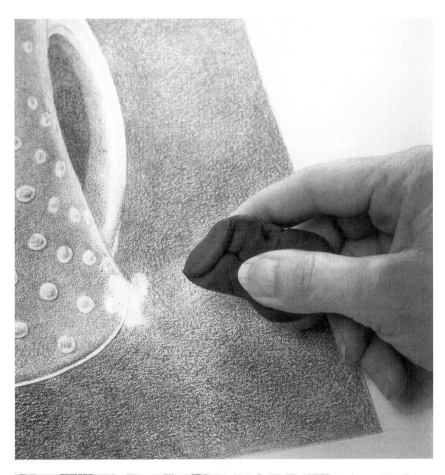

Erasing Small Details. The quickest way to erase a small detail is to over-erase—remove a wider area of pigment than seems necessary. Attempting to erase a tiny offending element is too time-consuming and fussy. Results are almost always quicker and cleaner when a whole small area is removed in one swoop and then restated.

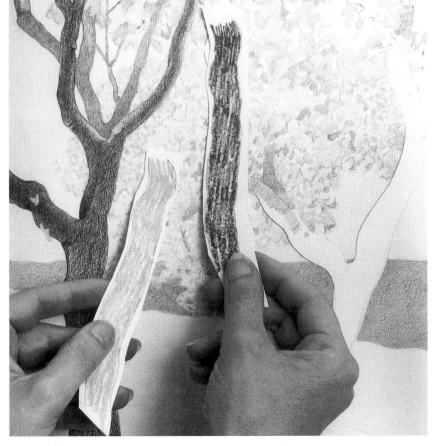

Color Decisions. Ideally, a drawing's colors are all worked out ahead of time. In practice, this is frequently not the case. When drawing stops because you can't decide what colors to use in a particular passage, try applying a few possible colors to scraps of paper in the approximate shape of the passage. Hold these up one by one to the area in question to see which will work best.

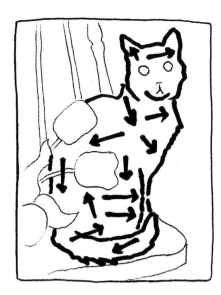

"Smoothing" Dark Areas. *Good tonal coverage is often achieved by applying a color layer with strokes that go in many directions (see diagram above). When you use firm pressure and dark colors, the result may be an overworked look due to too many multidirectional tracks and trails. These conflicting stroke marks can be "smoothed away" by stroking the area lightly in one direction only with the last pencil used (see photo and sketch at right). This stroking is not intended to physically smooth the surface, nor to add color, but merely to organize the short nap of the surface for an even sheen.*

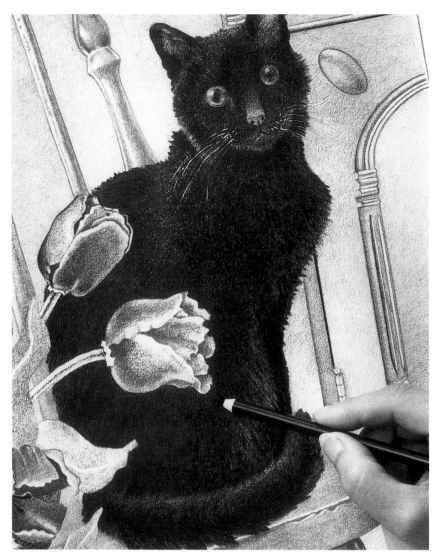

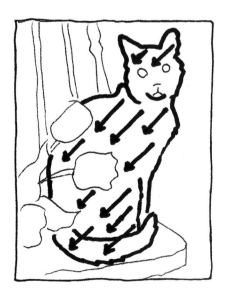

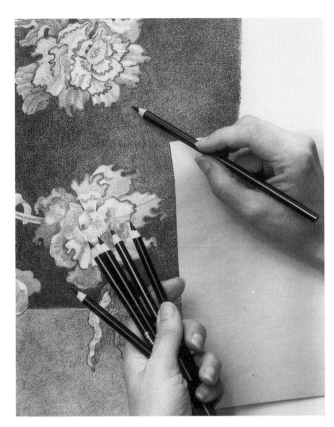

Working on Backgrounds. *It is sometimes a good idea, when drawing a large negative space, to work with five or six sharp pencils of the same color. This eliminates the need to resharpen a single pencil every few moments—a task that can make drawing "feel" too slow. It can also help keep your concentration steady when drawing a particularly tough or complicated passage.*

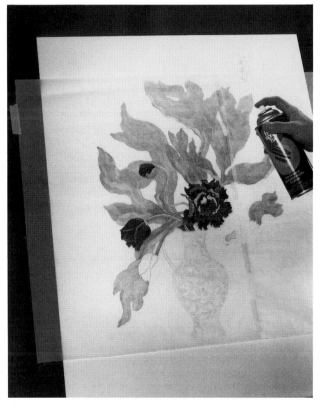

Intensifying Color. *Spraying a fixative incorrectly can accidentally and drastically intensify a drawing's colors. But this potential problem can also be put to a deliberate use. In this drawing, everything has been masked off except the flowers. Carefully spraying these with a fixative for a somewhat longer than normal time—about five seconds total—greatly intensifies their colors.*

18

STUDIO TIPS

Here are a few more time-saving suggestions. These deal with tools and materials in the studio or work space. But as artists, we all work differently. Your best time-saving strategies will ultimately result from looking more closely at your own working habits.

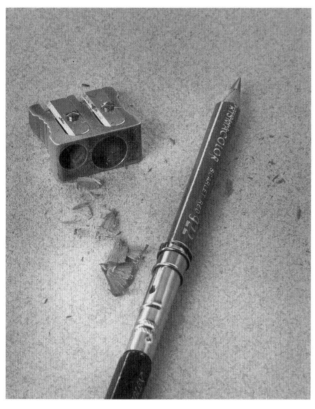

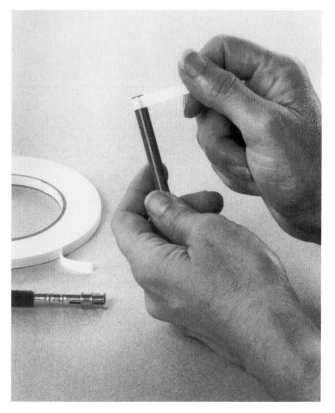

Sharpening Short Pencils. Pencil extenders can add a lot of mileage to pencils. But because a short stub of pencil tends to rotate in the ferrule of the extender, sharpening it almost always means first removing it. There is a simple way of correcting this time-wasting annoyance.

Add masking tape shims to the ends of short pencils before inserting them into extenders. A single layer of ¼-inch tape usually makes a tight enough fit to keep the pencil from turning inside the extender's ferrule while sharpening. A very short but taped pencil stub can also be pulled partly out of the ferrule for a slightly longer sharpening life.

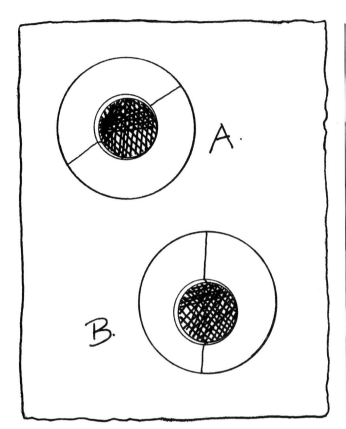

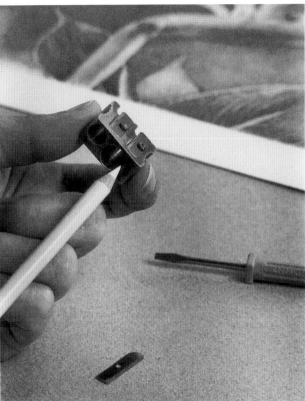

Broken Leads. *Pencil leads that break frequently can be very frustrating. A first step toward avoiding this nuisance is making sure that all the pencils you buy have well-centered leads (A). Avoid pencils with off-center leads (B) and those with shafts of half-dark/half-light wood, which tend to splinter and "hang up" in a sharpener.*

Another way of avoiding broken pencil leads is changing the blades of hand-held sharpeners more often. It shouldn't take more than a few easy twists to maintain a sharp point. And try using the larger of the sharpener's two openings. This removes less wood—and snagged wood is often the real cause of a broken lead.

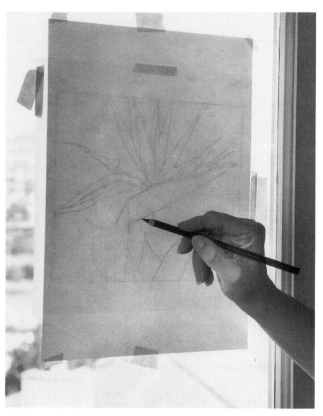

Transferring. During daylight hours, a window can often substitute for a too-small or unavailable light box. Simply tape up the preliminary tracing or drawing to be transferred, then tape a clean sheet of drawing paper over it.

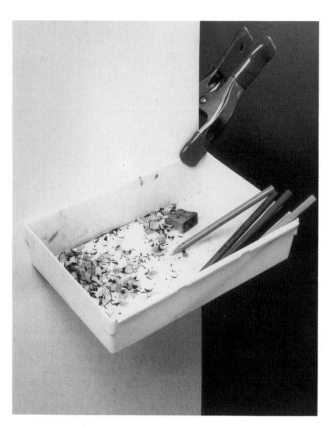

Sharpening on Location. When you are working at locations away from your studio taboret, or standing while working on large-format drawings, try clamping a pencil shavings holder nearby. A large spring-loaded hardware clamp makes this easy to do.

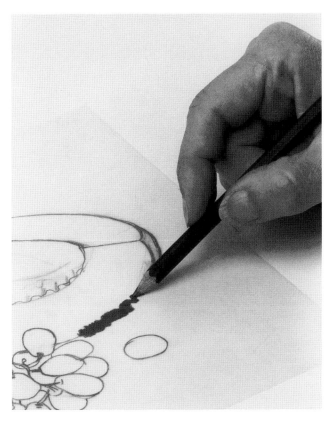

For transferring a preliminary drawing on tracing paper to a relatively thick board or to a colored paper, neither a light box nor a window will work. Instead, apply a dense coat of graphite on the reverse side of the preliminary drawing, covering only the guidelines. (An old Koh-I-Noor "Blackie" pencil, if you have one, is great for this. A more readily available alternative, the Derwent Graphic 9B, also provides a suitably dense stroke.) Position the tracing paper right side up on a clean drawing surface and lightly retrace the image. Lightness of retracing is important, so no impression except a faint line will be transferred to the clean sheet.

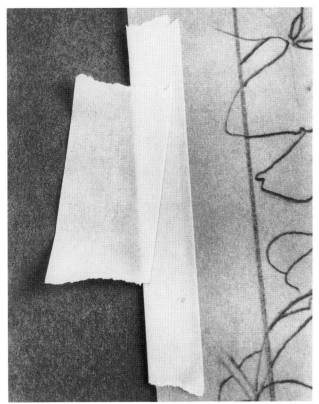

Tape on Tape. Because the tracing paper so heavily used and reused in the planning and transfer stages of drawing is fragile, if often gets torn as masking tape is used and removed. A good habit when starting with such a paper is to affix two or three short lengths of doubled-over masking tape along its edges. These provide sturdy, nontearable fastening places for new tape as needed.

Keeping Drawing Surfaces Clean.
Keeping a drawing board at a near-vertical position helps keep a drawing's margins, whites, and light values clean. Fine pigment particles will tend to fall away, rather than being ground in by your hand or the scratch sheet under it.

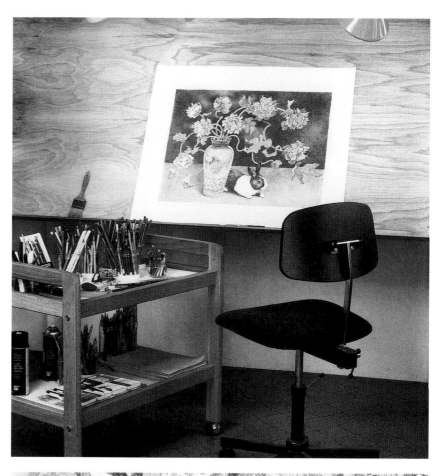

It helps also to keep a small utility brush (in this case a paint brush) nearby and to use it routinely for lightly brushing away pigment particles.

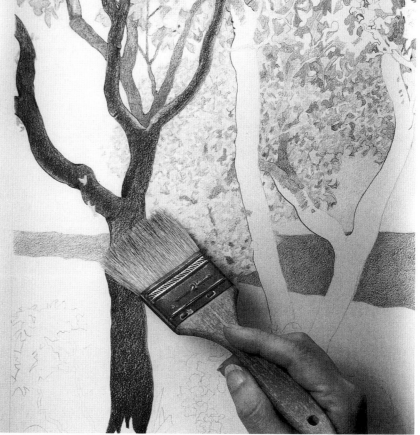

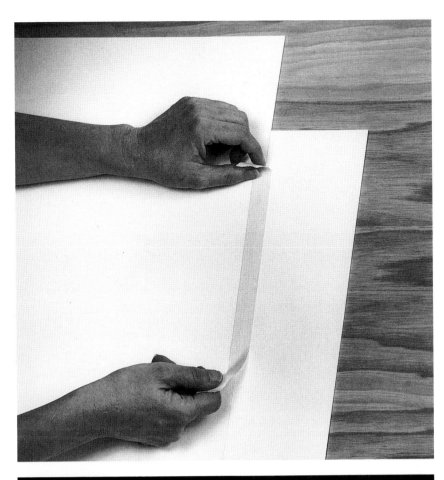

With large work and paper-white backgrounds it is often critical that the drawing surface be protected from scars or blemishes. It is helpful in this situation to attach a pair of side wings to the drawing paper or board. These panels—made of a thickness equal to the drawing surface and fastened with masking tape from the back as shown—are then grasped when the drawing must be moved, taped up for spraying, or otherwise handled.

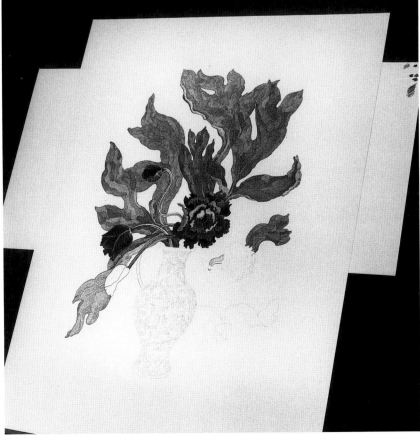

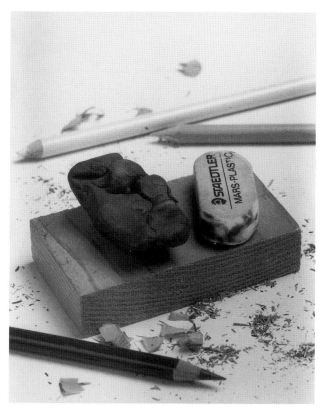

Erasers, especially kneaded erasers, can easily pick up particles of pigment from a taboret—and deposit them in a ruinous streak on a drawing's white passage or margin. This can be avoided by using a small block of wood (or a small box) as a raised surface for erasers, up out of any pigment dust.

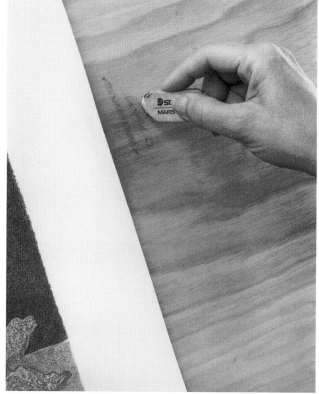

Spraying Fixative. It can be a dismaying surprise to spray a finished drawing with fixative—and see blotches of unwanted color appear in a margin. Because seemingly invisible pigment dust tends to darken and intensify with fixative, it is essential that even a visually clean finished margin be eraser-cleaned before spraying. Readying an eraser for this task can be quickly done with a few passes across the bare wood of a drawing board.

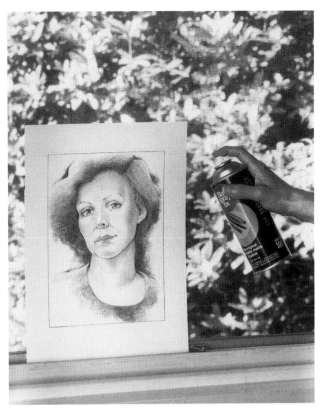

Spraying with Good Ventilation. It is very important that spraying of fixatives be done with proper ventilation. One way of achieving this is to position a drawing to be sprayed against the screen of an open window. If the drawing stands easily, or is sucked against the screen, excess spray will be carried outdoors. Should the drawing resist staying put, or push away from the screen, the airflow is wrong for spraying here. If no window works well, spray outdoors or quickly leave the room for awhile after spraying. The vapor of any spray fixative can be harmful, and its potential danger must not be underrated.

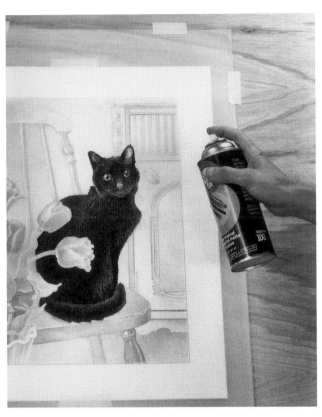

Despite any label directions to the contrary, it is always best to position colored pencil drawings vertically when spraying them, to avoid dripping solvent down onto them. It is also best (again contrary to label instructions) to spray with a few very light coats, rather than saturating a drawing (and probably drastically changing its colors). And for colored pencil work generally, only the dark or heavy pressure areas need spraying. The rest of a drawing (such as that shown with the cat) can be masked off with tracing paper.

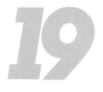

AN ALTERNATIVE TO WHITE-PENCIL BURNISHING

Among the unique properties of colored pencils is their ability to produce a painted as well as a drawn appearance. And it is to achieve the painterly look of colored pencils that an extremely time-consuming technique has developed. This is a method called white-pencil burnishing.

The technique works like this: Pencil color is applied to bristol board with medium pressure. A white or very light-valued pencil is then used with heavy pressure over the entire paper surface, mashing or compressing color and paper tooth together for a smooth, glazed look. Each succeeding layer of color is also heavily burnished in this manner. The motive is to blend and lighten colors and at the same time seal the paper's surface for an unflecked, painted appearance.

However, white-pencil burnishing is an enormously slow way of working. Similar effects can be achieved with the far faster and more straightforward approach of merely switching to a more pliant surface (or film) and using heavy pencil pressure as color is applied. The softer drawing surface is thus glazed and sealed with *color* rather than a heavily pressed-on *white*. A white pencil in this swifter technique is used only to lighten color, never as a wholesale treatment applied across an entire drawing.

To see the differences and similarities, consider the following examples of white-pencil burnishing and an alternative method.

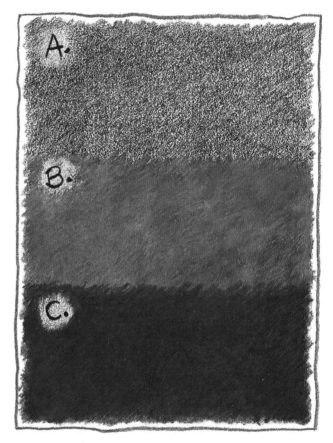

White-Pencil Burnishing. *In this example, a 906 Copenhagen Blue pencil was tonally applied with medium pressure to a bristol board surface, filling the rectangle. This layer can be seen in area A. With a white pencil and heavy pressure, the remainder of the rectangle was burnished, flattening the paper tooth and sealing the surface, as seen in area B. Finally, the blue was again applied over the white pencil in area C. (In this technique, these last two steps are usually repeated with each subsequent layer of color.)*

A Faster Way. For this example, a softer paper was used—two-ply Rising museum board—and the color was applied with heavy pressure, with no white-pencil burnishing.

A 903 True Blue (shown lightly applied for comparison at the top of the rectangle) was applied tonally using heavy pressure. This easily flattened the softer paper tooth and sealed the surface. It required but a fraction of the time needed for the burnished example and resulted in a less waxy finished surface. (The lighter blue pencil was used to better match the final result of a darker blue mixed with white in the burnished example.)

An Even Faster Way. Here a sheet of Cronaflex—a translucent, Mylar-like film—was used instead of a paper surface. A 903 True Blue was again applied but now with only moderate pressure. This translucent material offers an extremely fast-working surface, yielding densely saturated areas of color almost effortlessly with no further burnishing or other manipulation needed.

Step-by-Step
COMPARING TWO TECHNIQUES

On these two pages, a five-step white-pencil burnishing technique is compared with a more direct
two-step alternative technique for achieving similar results.

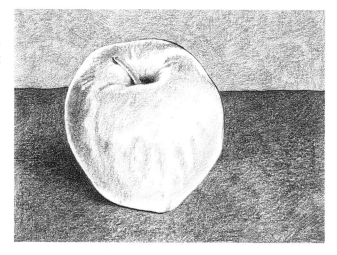

Step One. *Various pencil colors
were applied, using light to medium pressure. Flecks of white paper remain very visible.*

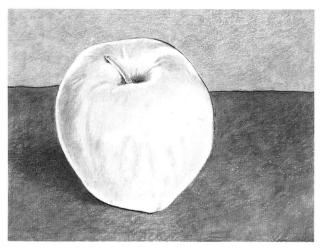

Step Two. *A white pencil was used with heavy pressure over the entire surface. This has altered the
colors and greatly reduced the visible white flecks.*

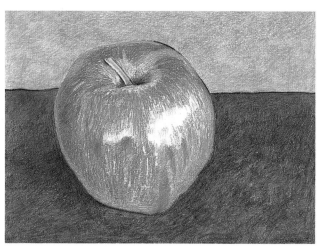

Step Three. *Another layer of pencil colors was applied over the glazed and whitened surface. This has
restored much of the color lost to the white pencil,
but some paper texture still shows.*

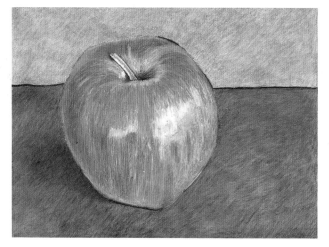

Step Four. *The white pencil was again used over the
entire surface to burnish away any remaining visible
paper texture. The surface now has a painterly look.*

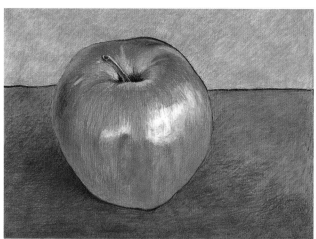

Step Five. *For a final, bolder result, colors were
again applied over the waxy surface to restore lost
saturation and to eliminate all traces of paper grain.*

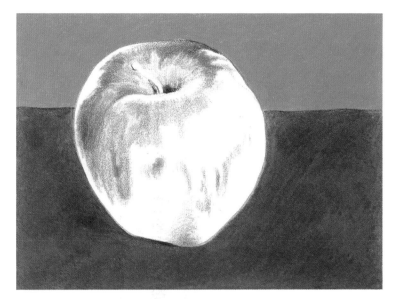

Step One. *For a second and very much faster method, a soft and pliant surface of Rising museum board was used, and the initial pencil colors were applied firmly to background and tabletop. Colors within the apple were applied with less pressure because they will only subtly mix with the next layer. Paper grain has been significantly reduced right from the beginning. Compare this with the first step in the white-pencil burnishing method.*

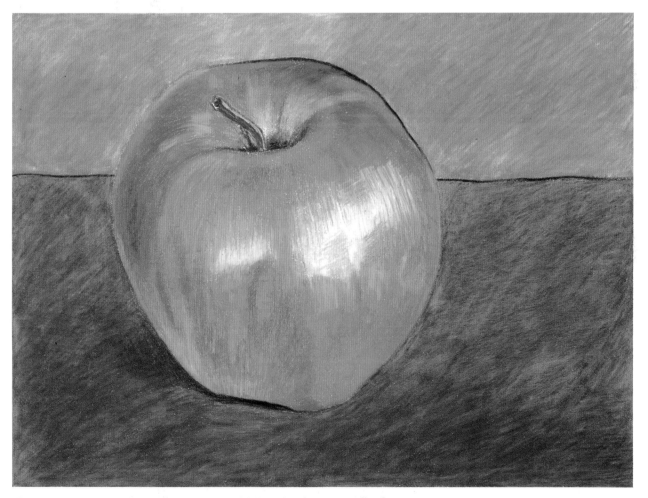

Step Two. *To complete the drawing, additional colors were firmly applied over the previous colors as needed. White was used in only two limited ways: to lighten the background and to develop and blend highlights. The drawing's painted effect was achieved by simply using firm pencil pressure to reduce paper grain while mixing the colors. Because the finished surface had fewer layers and thus was less waxy, colors could in every case be more easily mixed. And because no white burnishing was used, the final colors appear more saturated.*

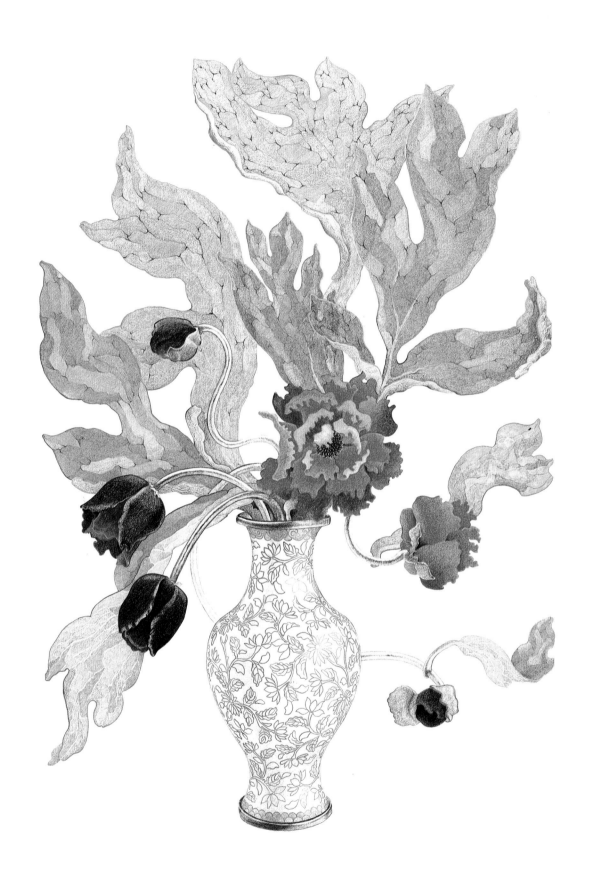

20

DISCOVERING HIDDEN TIME TRAPS

There is another way of speeding our work, one we haven't yet discussed. It involves hidden time traps—those work habits that seem to be furthering a drawing's progress but are actually slowing it down. These stalling habits, which we all occasionally fall prey to, can add extra hours or even days to our work on a drawing.

Hidden time traps are not to be confused with the rituals artists often find necessary before setting out on any new creative journey. Tidying up a work area, sharpening every pencil in sight, pacing about—these types of "make-ready" action are merely the warming up to a task at hand. Our hidden time traps involve subtle things we do in the process of drawing, not beforehand, and often look more like honest work than deliberate delay. Some examples are excessive layering, over-refining of negative space, or gravitating always to a drawing's "safe" areas to work. We can best combat such habits by discovering the uncertainties that cause them.

Confronting Uncertainties
There are many negative feelings about the word *confrontation*. It sounds aggressive and unpleasant, and maybe suggestive of trouble. But for our purposes, it can be a wonderful word. For what *confronting* really means, after all, is merely standing face to face with a situation. And that is exactly what we must do. We must very squarely face, early on, whatever we are most unsure of.

A frank realization that we are using stalling tactics can sometimes trigger the realization of what it is we are avoiding. We may, for instance, feel slightly reluctant to render a complicated form, to handle a chancy background, or to change a color we are beginning to suspect is wrong. We may even experience a dawning fear that the paper itself is not right for the piece now half-finished on it and ought to be changed. But whatever the problem, to resolve it we must confront and describe it. We must put our real reason for slowing down into specific words.

Finding a Description
It is said that artists must be good observers. The usual interpretation of this is that we must be able to see all the large and small things about a form or a scene. But this may not be the whole story. It may be equally important that we also be sharp observers of all that is happening to a drawing as work on it progresses. Acquiring this kind of objective observation is sometimes difficult, but it can be learned.

We take a giant step in this direction when we realize that if our work unaccountably slows down, it is probably because we are dodging one component by working too much at others. To pinpoint what is being avoided—sometimes an elusive task—try seeing a whole drawing as its barest components—the issues we all must face with each piece we start. These are:

1. Basic idea

2. Composition

3. Draftsmanship

4. Color

5. Textural character

6. Mood

7. Unity

Ask yourself, as you sift through these essential components, if each is working effectively. Describe clearly and verbally to yourself what each component is (or is not) supposed to do. Include this seven-part list in your silent dialogue, and be prepared to confront any problem areas in it immediately.

A final irony about the whole subject of hidden time traps is that the problem we try to avoid often relates to the very reason we started the work in the first place. It is what excited and motivated us. All that we are really confronting, therefore, are the vital and positive links to the things that first engaged us.

FLAME BOUQUET
Colored pencil on Rising museum board,
24" x 32" (61.0 x 81.3 cm).
Collection of the artist.

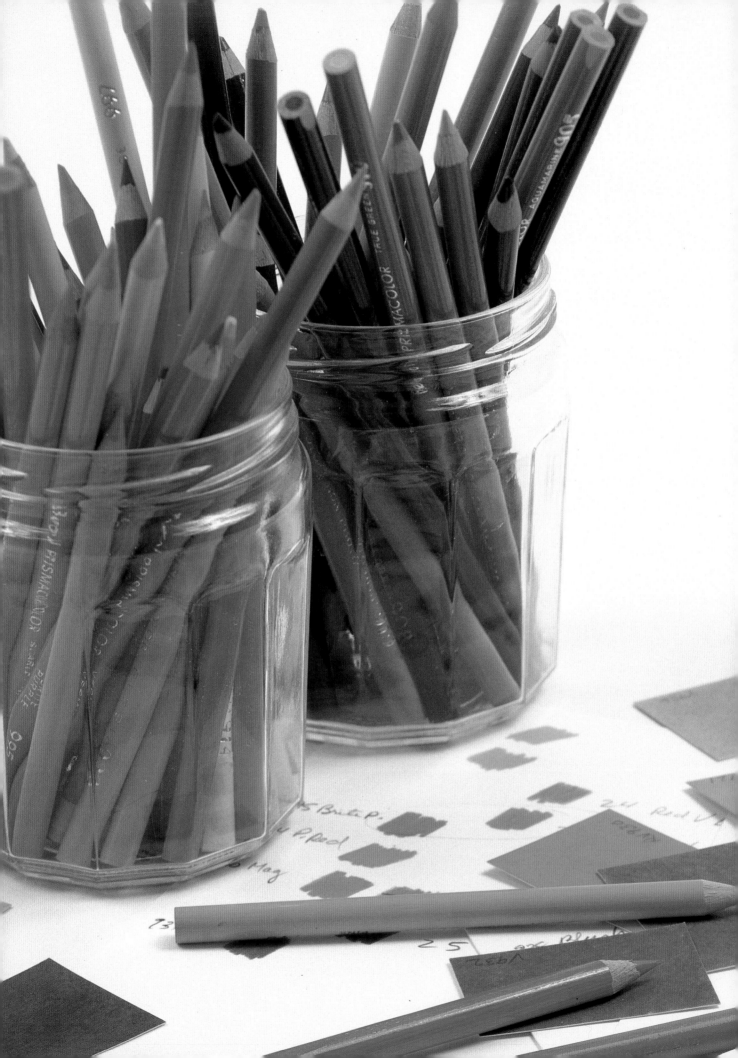

APPENDIXES

APPENDIX A

Hue–Value–Intensity Charts for Prismacolor Pencils

In the charts on the following pages, all the Prismacolor colored pencils are shown systematically organized and positioned according to each pencil's hue, value, and intensity. Determinations of these three dimensions were made by using each pencil at full strength (with heavy pressure) on a good quality white paper, then viewing the results under a mixture of ambient daylight and incandescent light.

Every effort was made to ensure accuracy, and I believe any aberrances to be slight. But it must be remembered that all color discrimination is to some degree a subjective matter.

When two pencil colors arrive at the same position (box) on a chart, both names are listed, but the closer of the two to that position is represented in the box and listed first. It should also be noted that inks used in printing do not always perfectly match pencil colors. But it is not the represented color that is essential, it is that pencil color's assigned position.

The Hue Scale. The hue for each chart is listed at the top and follows the traditional twelve-hue color wheel (see diagram). All reddish colored pencils, for example, appear on the Red chart, and comprise the red family. Reddish-violet pencils appear on the Red-Violet chart, and so on.

Some colored pencils appear to truly bridge two separate hue families. One of these is 997 Beige, which falls somewhere between orange and yellow-orange. Deciding where to place such colors was done by seeing how well they appear to belong with other members of the two families. The 997 Beige seems by this method to coexist more comfortably with the Yellow-Orange group than with Orange. A bridging pencil of this kind is denoted by having the initials of its alternate hue family in parentheses after its own name.

The Value Scale. The nine-step value scale for each chart is designed to be read vertically, beginning with black at the bottom and gradually lightening to white at the top. More or fewer steps are sometimes used to express a range of values, but in this case a medium value with three usable steps above it and three below (between white and black) seems adequate.

Again, some pencil colors fall between these listed value steps. One example is 920 True Green, neither clearly a Medium High nor a High. In this, and other such cases, the value position selected is the closer of the two. A plus or minus sign in parentheses following a color's name indicates that its true value is probably slightly above or below its assigned position.

The Intensity Scale. The intensity scale exists horizontally on each chart and contains seven steps ranging from Very Weak to Very Strong. These designations refer to a pencil color's purity of hue, as experienced visually.

It is this dullness/brightness scale that is perhaps the most subjective of the three scales used. For these charts, each pencil's intensity position was determined by relating and comparing it with all the other pencils, as well as with its own family members. A green, therefore, that may be the most intense in its own family will still not be rated as bright as the most intense of the yellows.

Using These Charts. A color wheel illustrates the relationships among its hues. Blue-violet, for example, is shown to be complementary to yellow-orange and analogous to blue-green. The charts on these pages are much more specific: They not only relate pencil colors by name to one another but do so by value and intensity as well as hue.

What this means is that if you are planning a composition using near-complements, you can first select your hues from the color wheel, then quickly find the names and numbers of appropriate pencils from the charts.

Should you want to juxtapose single layers of analogous colors and also match them in intensity, you can consult hue charts that are near one another and from these select colors of similar intensity. In this way, hours of testing colors might be saved.

The value designations of these charts offer still another kind of aid—particularly when you are working with heavy-pressure techniques. Ordinarily, a pencil's value is more or less controlled by hand pressure when drawing. But to achieve the saturated look of painting with colored pencils, a constant heavy pencil pressure is needed to produce each pencil's darkest value. Pencil values on the charts, having been arrived at with heavy pressure, offer the artist a very fast way of checking any pencil's value position before use.

Seeing colors presented as they are in these charts can also provide an interesting overview of the nature of the various Prismacolor hue families. All the blues, for example, can be seen to lean toward blue-green. There are no medium nor very low values of yellow. Red and violet contain the most dark colors—but not the darkest. The darkest is a blue, and the brightest color is a yellow.

And you can, if you like, add by hand other brands of colored pencils to these charts. If you use the Prismacolor pencils already charted as a guide, the assignment of positions for other pencils can be a fairly straightforward process.

A Twelve-Hue Color Wheel

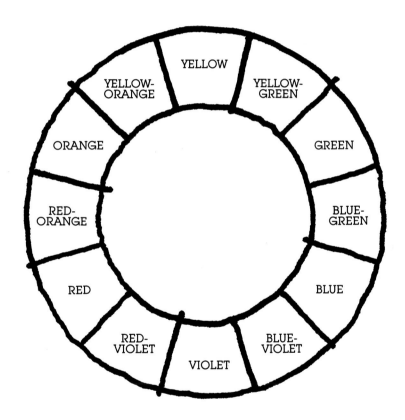

RED

	VERY WEAK	WEAK	MEDIUM WEAK	MEDIUM	MEDIUM STRONG	STRONG	VERY STRONG
WHITE							
VERY HIGH							
HIGH			928 Blush (−)				
MEDIUM HIGH				929 Pink (R-V)	926 Carmine (−)		
MEDIUM						923 Scarlet Lake	
MEDIUM LOW			937 Tuscan Red		925 Crimson Lake (+)	924 Crimson Red (+)	
LOW							
VERY LOW							
BLACK							

VALUE

INTENSITY

RED-ORANGE

	VERY WEAK	WEAK	MEDIUM WEAK	MEDIUM	MEDIUM STRONG	STRONG	VERY STRONG
WHITE							
VERY HIGH							
HIGH							
MEDIUM HIGH						921 Vermilion Red	
MEDIUM						922 Scarlet Red	
MEDIUM LOW				944 Terra Cotta			
LOW							
VERY LOW							
BLACK							

VALUE

INTENSITY

ORANGE

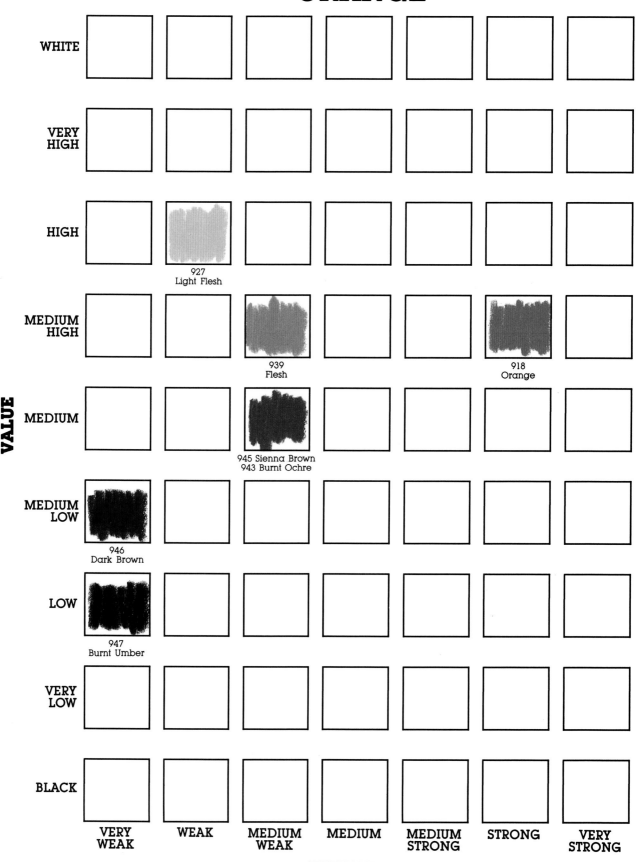

VALUE

WHITE

VERY HIGH

HIGH
927
Light Flesh

MEDIUM HIGH
939
Flesh
918
Orange

MEDIUM
945 Sienna Brown
943 Burnt Ochre

MEDIUM LOW
946
Dark Brown

LOW
947
Burnt Umber

VERY LOW

BLACK

VERY WEAK · WEAK · MEDIUM WEAK · MEDIUM · MEDIUM STRONG · STRONG · VERY STRONG

INTENSITY

YELLOW-ORANGE

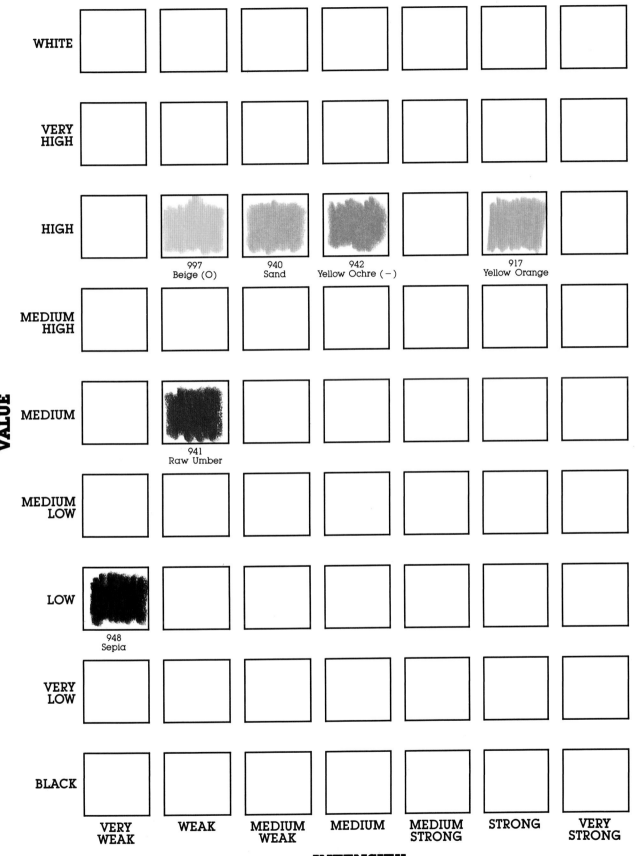

WHITE

VERY HIGH

HIGH
- 997 Beige (O)
- 940 Sand
- 942 Yellow Ochre (−)
- 917 Yellow Orange

MEDIUM HIGH

MEDIUM
- 941 Raw Umber

MEDIUM LOW

LOW
- 948 Sepia

VERY LOW

BLACK

VALUE

INTENSITY

VERY WEAK · WEAK · MEDIUM WEAK · MEDIUM · MEDIUM STRONG · STRONG · VERY STRONG

YELLOW

	VERY WEAK	WEAK	MEDIUM WEAK	MEDIUM	MEDIUM STRONG	STRONG	VERY STRONG
WHITE							
VERY HIGH		914 Cream (+)				915 Lemon Yellow (+)	916 Canary Yellow
HIGH							
MEDIUM HIGH							
MEDIUM							
MEDIUM LOW							
LOW							
VERY LOW							
BLACK							

VALUE

INTENSITY

YELLOW-GREEN

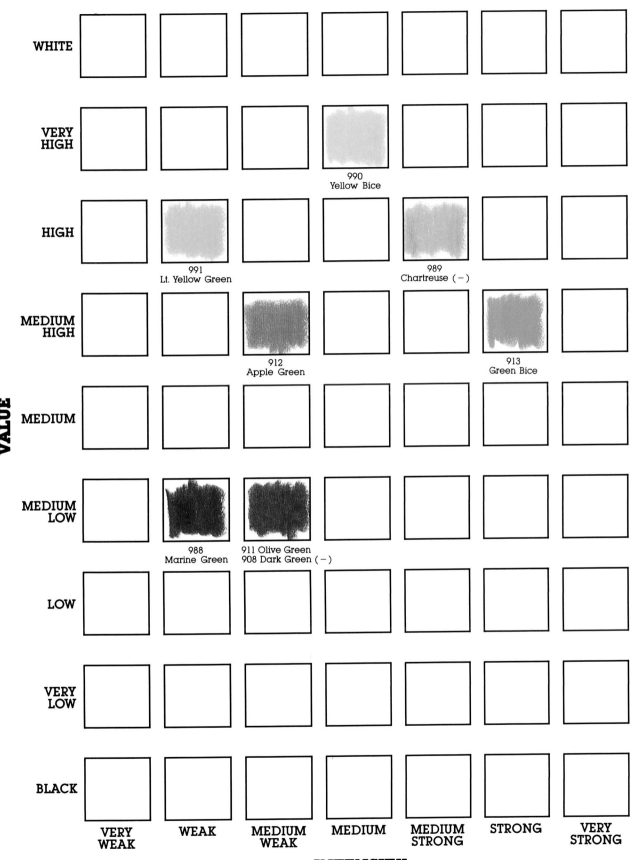

VALUE

WHITE

VERY HIGH
990
Yellow Bice

HIGH
991
Lt. Yellow Green
989
Chartreuse (−)

MEDIUM HIGH
912
Apple Green
913
Green Bice

MEDIUM

MEDIUM LOW
988
Marine Green
911 Olive Green
908 Dark Green (−)

LOW

VERY LOW

BLACK

| VERY WEAK | WEAK | MEDIUM WEAK | MEDIUM | MEDIUM STRONG | STRONG | VERY STRONG |

INTENSITY

GREEN

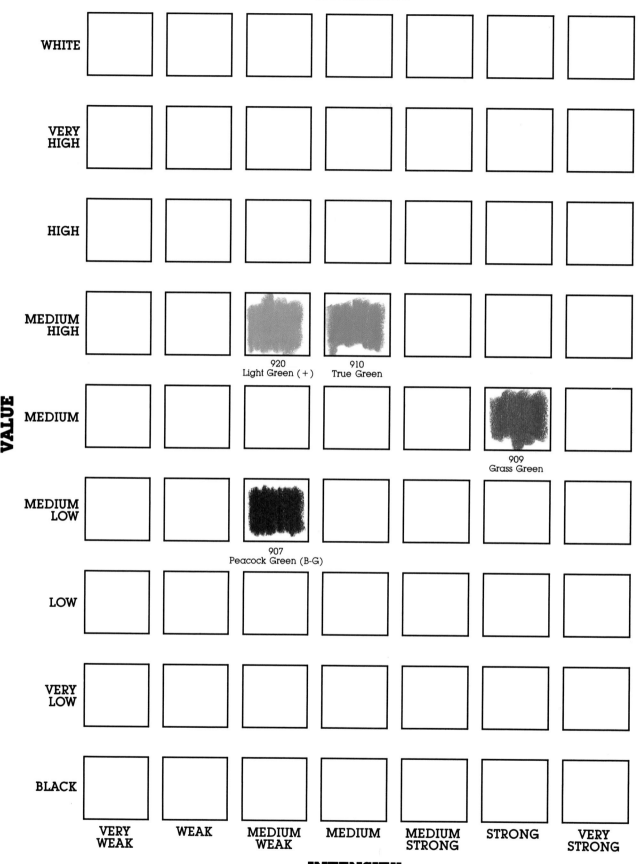

VALUE

WHITE

VERY HIGH

HIGH

MEDIUM HIGH

920
Light Green (+)

910
True Green

MEDIUM

909
Grass Green

MEDIUM LOW

907
Peacock Green (B-G)

LOW

VERY LOW

BLACK

VERY WEAK · WEAK · MEDIUM WEAK · MEDIUM · MEDIUM STRONG · STRONG · VERY STRONG

INTENSITY

BLUE-GREEN

VALUE

	VERY WEAK	WEAK	MEDIUM WEAK	MEDIUM	MEDIUM STRONG	STRONG	VERY STRONG
WHITE							
VERY HIGH							
HIGH							
MEDIUM HIGH			992 Light Aqua				
MEDIUM				905 Aquamarine			
MEDIUM LOW							
LOW							
VERY LOW							
BLACK							

INTENSITY

BLUE

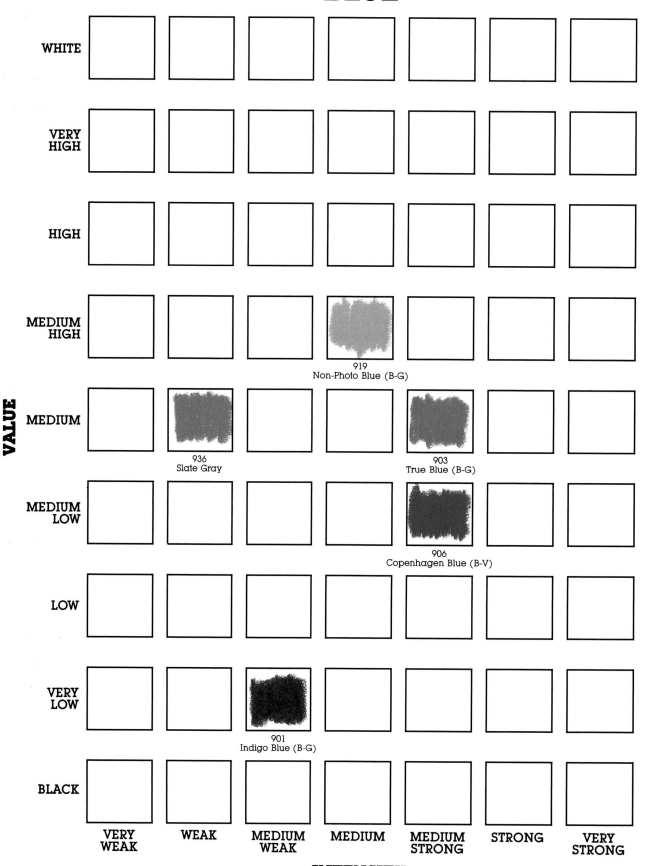

VALUE

	VERY WEAK	WEAK	MEDIUM WEAK	MEDIUM	MEDIUM STRONG	STRONG	VERY STRONG
WHITE							
VERY HIGH							
HIGH							
MEDIUM HIGH			919 Non-Photo Blue (B-G)				
MEDIUM		936 Slate Gray			903 True Blue (B-G)		
MEDIUM LOW					906 Copenhagen Blue (B-V)		
LOW							
VERY LOW			901 Indigo Blue (B-G)				
BLACK							

INTENSITY

BLUE-VIOLET

VALUE

	VERY WEAK	WEAK	MEDIUM WEAK	MEDIUM	MEDIUM STRONG	STRONG	VERY STRONG
WHITE							
VERY HIGH							
HIGH							
MEDIUM HIGH				904 Light Blue			
MEDIUM							
MEDIUM LOW						902 Ultramarine / 999 Brite Blue Violet (+)	
LOW				933 Blue Violet			
VERY LOW							
BLACK							

INTENSITY

VIOLET

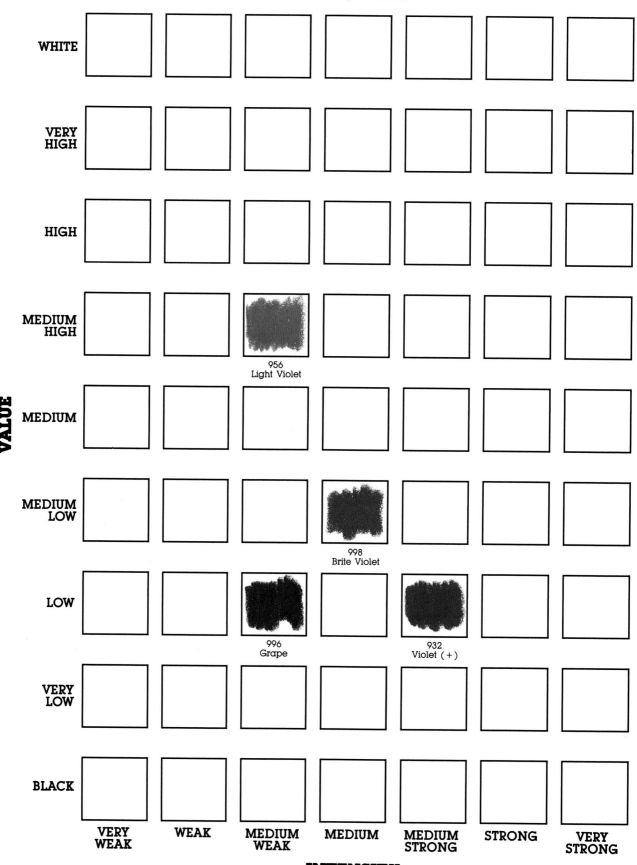

VALUE

WHITE

VERY HIGH

HIGH

MEDIUM HIGH
956
Light Violet

MEDIUM

MEDIUM LOW
998
Brite Violet

LOW
996
Grape
932
Violet (+)

VERY LOW

BLACK

VERY WEAK · WEAK · MEDIUM WEAK · MEDIUM · MEDIUM STRONG · STRONG · VERY STRONG

INTENSITY

RED-VIOLET

	VERY WEAK	WEAK	MEDIUM WEAK	MEDIUM	MEDIUM STRONG	STRONG	VERY STRONG
WHITE							
VERY HIGH							
HIGH							
MEDIUM HIGH				993 Hot Pink 934 Lavender			
MEDIUM					995 Brite Purple	930 Magenta 994 Process Red	
MEDIUM LOW							
LOW					931 Purple		
VERY LOW							
BLACK							

VALUE

INTENSITY

WARM GRAYS

COLD GRAYS

VALUE	WARM GRAYS	COLD GRAYS
WHITE		
VERY HIGH		
HIGH	964 Warm Grey Very Light	968 Cold Grey Very Light
MEDIUM HIGH	963 Warm Grey Light	967 Cold Grey Light
MEDIUM		
MEDIUM LOW	962 Warm Grey Medium	966 Cold Grey Medium
LOW	961 Warm Grey Dark	965 Cold Grey Dark
VERY LOW	935 Black	
BLACK		

APPENDIX B

Relative Waxiness of Prismacolor Art Stix and Pencils

All Prismacolor pencils and Art Stix contain some degree of softness or waxiness. It is this quality, in fact, that allows these drawing tools to glide smoothly across a drawing surface. But because each color is separately formulated, the degree of waxiness from one to another is not always the same.

In this chart, the Prismacolor pencils and sticks are organized by hue into three degrees as least, medium, and most waxy. None of these categories is to be taken as better or worse than another, but merely as quickly accessible information for those whose personal techniques and uses thrive best on minimum or maximum waxiness.

PRISMACOLOR ART STIX (48 COLORS)

HUE FAMILY	LEAST WAXY	MEDIUM WAXY	MOST WAXY
Red	1924 Crimson Red	1923 Crimson Lake	1926 Carmine Red 1928 Blush 1929 Pink
Red Orange		1921 Vermilion Red 1922 Scarlet Red 1944 Terra Cotta	
Orange		1918 Orange 1943 Burnt Ochre 1945 Sienna Brown 1946 Dark Brown 1947 Burnt Umber	1927 Light Flesh 1939 Flesh
Yellow-Orange	1941 Raw Umber 1948 Sepia	1940 Sand 1942 Yellow Ochre	1917 Yellow-Orange
Yellow			1914 Cream 1915 Lemon Yellow 1916 Canary Yellow
Yellow-Green	1908 Dark Green 1911 Olive Green		1912 Apple Green 1913 Green Bice
Green	1907 Peacock Green	1909 Grass Green	1910 True Green
Blue-Green			1905 Aquamarine
Blue	1901 Indigo Blue 1906 Copenhagen Blue	1903 True Blue 1919 Non-Photo Blue	1936 Slate Gray
Blue-Violet	1933 Blue Violet		1902 Ultramarine 1904 Light Blue
Violet	1932 Violet		
Red-Violet	1931 Purple	1930 Magenta	1934 Lavender
Neutral, Metallic	1935 Black 1949 Silver 1950 Gold 1951 Copper		1938 White

PRISMACOLOR PENCILS (72 COLORS)

HUE FAMILY	LEAST WAXY	MEDIUM WAXY	MOST WAXY
Red		923 Scarlet Lake 924 Crimson Red 925 Crimson Lake 937 Tuscan Red	926 Carmine Red 928 Blush 929 Pink
Red Orange	944 Terra Cotta	921 Vermilion Red 922 Scarlet Red	
Orange	947 Burnt Umber	943 Burnt Ochre 945 Sienna Brown 946 Dark Brown	918 Orange 927 Light Flesh 939 Flesh
Yellow-Orange		941 Raw Umber 948 Sepia	917 Yellow Orange 940 Sand 942 Yellow Ochre 997 Beige
Yellow			914 Cream 915 Lemon Yellow 916 Canary Yellow
Yellow-Green	988 Marine Green	908 Dark Green 911 Olive Green	912 Apple Green 913 Green Bice 989 Chartreuse 990 Yellow Bice 991 Lt. Yellow Green
Green	907 Peacock Green	909 Grass Green	910 True Green 920 Light Green
Blue-Green			905 Aquamarine 992 Light Aqua
Blue	901 Indigo Blue	903 True Blue 906 Copenhagen Blue 919 Non-Photo Blue	936 Slate Gray
Blue-Violet			902 Ultramarine 904 Light Blue 933 Blue Violet 999 Brite Blue Violet
Violet	996 Grape	932 Violet	956 Light Violet 998 Brite Violet
Red-Violet	931 Purple	930 Magenta 995 Brite Purple	934 Lavender 993 Hot Pink 994 Process Red
Neutral, Metallic	935 Black 949 Silver 950 Gold 951 Copper 961 Warm Grey Dark 965 Cold Grey Dark	962 Warm Grey Medium 966 Cold Grey Medium	938 White 963 Warm Grey Light 964 Warm Grey Very Light 967 Cold Grey Light 968 Cold Grey Very Light

APPENDIX C

A Cross-Reference Chart for Prismacolor and Derwent Pencils

Although none of the colors in these two pencil lines are perfectly matched, some are quite similar. These are represented by aligned color swatches.

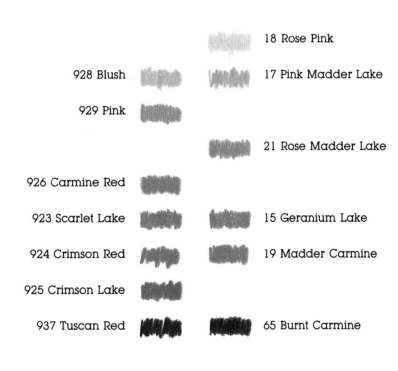

PRISMACOLOR	DERWENT

RED

	18 Rose Pink
928 Blush	17 Pink Madder Lake
929 Pink	
	21 Rose Madder Lake
926 Carmine Red	
923 Scarlet Lake	15 Geranium Lake
924 Crimson Red	19 Madder Carmine
925 Crimson Lake	
937 Tuscan Red	65 Burnt Carmine

RED-ORANGE

	13 Pale Vermilion
921 Vermilion Red	12 Scarlet Lake
922 Scarlet Red	14 Deep Vermilion
	64 Terra Cotta
944 Terra Cotta	

PRISMACOLOR	DERWENT

ORANGE

	16 Flesh Pink
927 Light Flesh	
939 Flesh	
	8 Middle Chrome
	9 Deep Chrome
918 Orange	10 Orange Chrome
	11 Spectrum Orange
	62 Burnt Sienna
943 Burnt Ochre	
945 Sienna Brown	63 Venetian Red
	61 Copper Beech
946 Dark Brown	
947 Burnt Umber	66 Chocolate

YELLOW-ORANGE

997 Beige	
917 Yellow-Orange	6 Deep Cadmium
	7 Naples Yellow
940 Sand	
942 Yellow Ochre	
	58 Raw Sienna
	60 Burnt Yellow Ochre
	57 Brown Ochre

PRISMACOLOR   DERWENT

YELLOW-ORANGE (cont.)

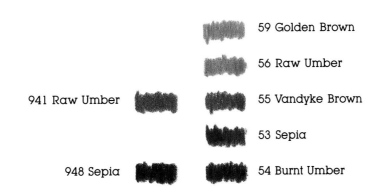

		59 Golden Brown
		56 Raw Umber
941 Raw Umber		55 Vandyke Brown
		53 Sepia
948 Sepia		54 Burnt Umber

YELLOW

914 Cream	
915 Lemon Yellow	1 Zinc Yellow
916 Canary Yellow	2 Lemon Cadmium
	4 Primrose Yellow
	5 Straw Yellow
	3 Gold

YELLOW-GREEN

990 Yellow Bice	
991 Light Yellow Green	
989 Chartreuse	
	48 May Green
913 Green Bice	47 Grass Green
912 Apple Green	
911 Olive Green	
	51 Olive Green

PRISMACOLOR   DERWENT

YELLOW-GREEN (cont.)

	52 Bronze
988 Marine Green	50 Cedar Green
908 Dark Green	49 Sap Green

GREEN

920 Light Green	44 Water Green
910 True Green	
	46 Emerald Green
909 Grass Green	
	45 Mineral Green
	42 Juniper Green
	43 Bottle Green
907 Peacock Green	

BLUE-GREEN

	39 Turquoise Blue
	40 Turquoise Green
992 Light Aqua	
	41 Jade Green
	38 Kingfisher Blue
905 Aquamarine	
	37 Oriental Blue

PRISMACOLOR   DERWENT

BLUE

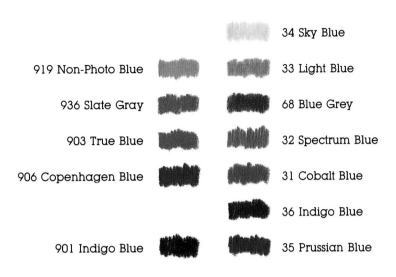

	34 Sky Blue
919 Non-Photo Blue	33 Light Blue
936 Slate Gray	68 Blue Grey
903 True Blue	32 Spectrum Blue
906 Copenhagen Blue	31 Cobalt Blue
	36 Indigo Blue
901 Indigo Blue	35 Prussian Blue

BLUE-VIOLET

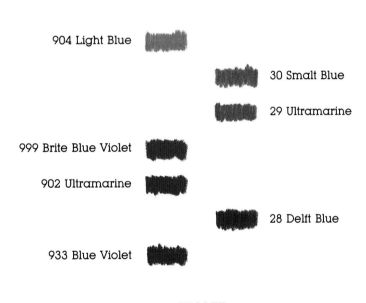

904 Light Blue	
	30 Smalt Blue
	29 Ultramarine
999 Brite Blue Violet	
902 Ultramarine	
	28 Delft Blue
933 Blue Violet	

VIOLET

956 Light Violet	26 Light Violet
	27 Blue Violet Lake
998 Brite Violet	
932 Violet	

PRISMACOLOR   DERWENT

VIOLET (cont.)

 25 Dark Violet

996 Grape

RED-VIOLET

934 Lavender

993 Hot Pink

 24 Red Violet Lake

995 Brite Purple   22 Magenta

994 Process Red

930 Magenta 20 Crimson Lake

25 Imperial Purple

931 Purple

NEUTRAL

938 White   72 Chinese White

71 Silver Grey

968 Cold Grey Very Light

964 Warm Grey Very Light

70 French Grey

967 Cold Grey Light

963 Warm Grey Light

69 Gunmetal

966 Cold Grey Medium

PRISMACOLOR   DERWENT

NEUTRAL (cont.)

962 Warm Grey Medium

965 Cold Grey Dark

961 Warm Grey Dark

935 Black   67 Ivory Black

METALLIC

949 Silver

950 Gold

951 Copper

INDEX

Edited by Brigid A. Mast
Designed by Jay Anning
Graphic production by Stanley Redfern